MICROCOSM PUBLISHING is Portland's most diversified publishing house and distributor, with a focus on the colorful, authentic, and empowering. Our books and zines have put your power in your hands since 1996, equipping readers to make positive changes in their lives and in the world around them. Microcosm emphasizes skill-building, showing hidden histories, and fostering creativity through challenging conventional publishing wisdom with books and bookettes about DIY skills, food, bicycling, gender, self-care, and social justice. What was once a distro and record label started by Joe Biel in a drafty bedroom was determined to be *Publishers Weekly*'s fastest-growing publisher of 2022 and #3 in 2023, and is now among the oldest independent publishing houses in Portland, OR, and Cleveland, OH. Biel is also the winner of PubWest's Innovator Award in 2024. We are a politically moderate, centrist publisher in a world that has inched to the right for the past 80 years.

Self-Care Won't Save Us

HOW TO FIGHT BURNOUT WITH SOLIDARITY AND SOCIAL CHANGE

CAROLINE MOORE

Microcosm Publishing
Portland, OR / Cleveland, OH

SELF-CARE WON'T SAVE US

How to Fight Burnout with Solidarity and Social Change
Part of the DIY Series

First Edition, 3,000 copies, first published January 13, 2026
ISBN 9781648412417
This is Microcosm # 734
Designed by Joe Biel and Sarah Koch
Edited by Ivy Zeller

For a catalog, write or visit:

Microcosm Publishing
2752 N Williams Ave.
Portland, OR 97227

All the news from the misfits in print at www.Microcosm.Pub/Newsletter.

Get more copies of this book at *www.Microcosm.Pub/SelfCareWontSaveUs*

EU Safety Information: microcosmpublishing.com/gpsr

To join the ranks of high-class stores that feature Microcosm titles, talk to your rep: In the U.S. COMO (Atlantic), ABRAHAM (Midwest), BOB BARNETT (Texas, Oklahoma, Arkansas, Louisiana), IMPRINT (Pacific), TURNAROUND (UK), UTP/MANDA (Canada), NEW-SOUTH (Australia/New Zealand), Observatoire (Africa, Europe), IPR (Middle East), APD (Asia), HarperCollins (India), and FAIRE in the gift trade.

Did you know that you can buy our books directly from us at sliding scale rates? Support a small, independent publisher and pay less than Amazon's price at www.Microcosm.Pub.

Global labor conditions are bad, and our roots in industrial Cleveland in the '70s and '80s made us appreciate the need to treat workers right. Therefore, our books are MADE IN THE USA.

Library of Congress Control Number: 2025027806

CONTENTS

INTRODUCTION

You're burned out. I mean, I don't know you personally. But since you've picked up this book, odds are good that you're feeling burned out. According to a report from Future Forum Pulse, a consortium that conducts research on workers' experience and expectations, 40% of us are feeling burned out, and that number rises to 48% among those under 30.[1] Odds are also good you've heard advice that you haven't found all that helpful—buy a candle, do some yoga, take a mental health day and a bubble bath, treat yourself. There's nothing wrong with doing those things of course. But they won't cure your burnout, because they are only treating the symptoms, not the cause.

To save ourselves from burnout, we have to look at what causes it. In the pages to come, we'll look at how hustle culture—our society's glorification of overwork—leads to burnout. We'll see how we got to where we are, and how we get to where we need to be.

Hustle culture, embracing an imagined moral duty to rise and grind even as it damages us, is a collective problem. Systemic problems require systemic solutions, and while there are some things that we can do independently, many of the needed changes require all of us. We need to not only save ourselves from burnout, but to save each other.

Freeing ourselves from the compulsion of overwork is a reachable goal. The work culture that we labor under produces

---

1 Future Forum Pulse Winter Snapshot Report, February 2023, futureforum.com/research/future-forum-pulse-winter-2022-2023-snapshot.

burnout, and our burnout robs us of the energy and resources to resist our own exploitation, so our work culture remains terrible. We need labor legislation, power, and leverage. To get those things, we need solidarity with each other and a belief in the idea that resistance is possible. We need leisure for solidarity, and we need solidarity for change.

This book is for anyone who needs to hear that their burnout is not their fault. It's also for those of you who might think that you aren't even really all that burned out. You couldn't possibly be burned out, you're making websites, not curing cancer.

But burnout isn't limited to high-stress environments; it comes for us all. It can be hard to even recognize when burnout starts, because it is a spectrum, not a black and white status. You aren't idealistic one day and cynical the next—it's a gradual slide. Burnout happens when you try to reconcile the disconnect between your expectations and your reality. You might expect your job to be fulfilling, but feel like you're just ticking boxes. Or you expect your career to allow time to live your actual life, but instead you barely have time to scrounge up dinner before you're ready for bed.

This is why a bubble bath or even a vacation can't fix it. When you return from a day or a week or a month away, the reality won't be any closer to your expectations when you return. A treat or a break can help alleviate the symptoms of burnout, and that's not a bad thing while we do the long-term work that needs to be done. But true self-care, really caring for ourselves and doing what's best for us as whole people, means fixing the root causes of burnout. Our burnout is built on the foundation of hustle culture.

Just like anyone else, I'm not immune to the siren call of hustle culture. I am speaking as someone who thought it was a reasonable idea to work a full-time job and start a business while struggling with a chronic illness. I thought that I could simply hustle my way out of being sick; instead, I ended up getting so sick that I had to file for FMLA to keep the full-time job.

Back then, I thought that hustling around the clock was the only way to run a business, because that's what I saw everyone else doing (at least, that's what they said they were doing). I worked so much, but still felt guilty any time I wasn't working. Our culture's morality about work, my fear about job scarcity, and every brand posting "rise and grind" inspired me to ignore my health until it crashed.

In the fifteen years since, I've learned how no one benefits from me working myself to death. That long hours don't serve us or the work we're trying to do. That putting in endless time goes against the way that our brains work. I've learned how the hustle model devalues people and encourages us to do that devaluing to ourselves. How our desire for meaning and identity in our work drives us.

But I've also learned how we can opt out and set boundaries around our work. Really live our lives instead of optimizing every second of them for maximum productivity. How we can really, truly care for ourselves and each other. I've learned that there are different ways to run a business, ones that might better align with our values and our needs. I've learned how important it is to recognize that we're in this together. I want to share those things with you, and that's why I wrote this book.

Everything in this book is not for everyone. Burnout is caused by many systemic problems, and in the same way that you can't save the entire Earth on your own by recycling some newspapers, there are limits to what you are able to do. You may read through the section on setting boundaries and think, *Sure, that's easy for you to say.*

You're right. It is significantly easier for some people to push back at work than it is for others—for people who are already marginalized, for people who absolutely cannot risk losing a job, for people whose employers simply don't care what they have to say. For this reason, I encourage those of you who can set boundaries to do so, because it doesn't only help you, it helps those who can't.

Driving changes in your work culture makes a difference for every person who works there. Do the things you're able to do, out of solidarity for everyone. Use any privilege that you do have, and understand that others are simply not in the same boat as you.

If some of this advice doesn't hit for you, if it isn't something you're able to do, that's okay. Maybe one day it will be. For now, the knowledge that you don't deserve to be ground down into a fine powder just to be able to cover rent is part of the battle.

If you only come away from this book with one thing, I hope it is this—a sincere belief that you have dignity, that every person has dignity, regardless of whether you work or not. A belief that our lives have meaning entirely separate from work, from productivity, from our ability to earn money. A belief that we are all in this together.

PART 1: HOW HUSTLE CULTURE LEADS TO BURNOUT

Hustle culture makes demands of us that are damaging to our bodies, our brains, and our social relationships. It affects how we view our work and worth. In this first part of the book, we will look at how our culture came to be so focused on hustling, the direct line from these views to our burnout epidemic, and how the way we work conflicts with the way that our brains function. After I tell you how and why everything is terrible, part two will focus on how we can unite against hustle culture, questions to ask for a burnout revolution, and how we save both ourselves and each other.

J. PALMER.

Chapter 1: What's So Bad about Hustle Culture Anyway?

Why am I so hard on hustle culture? What's so bad about it anyway? First, we need to look at what hustle culture is and what it is not.

Many may read my criticisms of hustle culture as a criticism of work itself, that those who don't want to commit to the constant grind lack work ethic or ambition. I'm not against work as a concept, or even against hard work. I've done plenty of it myself. What I am against is a culture that promotes not hard work, but relentless work.

Hustle culture tells us that being busy is the same as being productive, the same as being successful. It tells us that we should prioritize work above every other thing in our lives, and if we don't, then we must not really want to achieve our goals. That if you aren't always working—always—then you must not want to succeed.

In so doing, hustle culture minimizes the things that matter in our lives outside of work, like rest, hobbies, personal relationships, and community. It tells us that if we aren't successful, it's our fault, even though our individual effort can never overcome systemic inequality. Hustle culture glorifies jobs that require long hours, and these types of jobs systemically push out caregivers and the disabled, while opportunities like unpaid internships are out of reach for lower-income people who can't afford to work for free.

We've been told that work is a meritocracy, that all of us—no matter our background—have the same opportunity to succeed by just grinding with the resources we already have. But this doesn't align with the reality we're seeing, and inequality can't be overcome by simply hustling harder. Hustle culture devalues people who can't, or don't want to, devote every bit of their lives to work. It devalues those of us who reject the idea that to be successful and do work with meaning, we have to be working at all times.

In short, hustle culture leads to burnout because it is an unrealistic and unsustainable set of ideals. The truth is, it's not only bad for us—physically, culturally, and emotionally. Overwork is a terrible way to produce anything of value, because it is in direct conflict with the way that our brains are built to work.

It Is Not How Our Brains Work

The human brain is an absolute marvel. Through our subconscious, the brain offers up solutions to complex problems while we drive to the coffee shop. It builds memories while we sleep—all while it holds our childhood phone numbers and the lyrics to our favorite songs.

But our brains require things from us to function well, and one of the most essential things our brains need to work is downtime. Your brain can't plow through twelve hours of work with no breaks; it works in short periods of highly effective output. Like a HIIT workout, you're putting in maximum effort, but you can only do it for a short time. Breaks help you recover from mental fatigue, while psychological distance from a task lets you remember the big picture. You couldn't roll a boulder up a hill for ten hours straight with no loss in productivity, and you can't do mental labor for that long without consequences either. To do thoughtful work, we need space to rest, and we can't get that space if we're filling our every second with work.

This is not new information that I have just discovered independently; we have known for a long time that brains need downtime to function. Our brains are complex things. Different work will fire up different parts of your brain, and you may think that your brain would be the most active when you're working. It isn't. Large parts of your brain light up when you're daydreaming, including the brain's executive network, which is the area we associate with solving problems and being creative. Psychologists used to think that these areas of the brain were dormant when we were daydreaming, but a study from the University of British Columbia found that daydreaming is a very active process, noting activity in many different regions of the brain while the mind wandered.[2] When we decrease the time that we're actively concentrating, we're actually increasing the time that our brains can spend solving problems. These regular breaks are also crucial to decrease our stress and sense of overwhelm, which is difficult in a culture that celebrates both.

The way that most of us work, spending eight hours at our desks, isn't really optimized for getting the best from our brains. The truth is, we really don't work for eight hours a day, and it's because we can't. The average employee in the UK self-reports only working for about three hours out of their eight-hour day, according to a 2016 survey of two thousand office workers performed by Vouchercloud. They spend the rest of their hours reading news, eating, or socializing.[3]

One view of that survey could be that people are incredibly lazy, frittering away their time on the company's dime. But social psychologist Devon Price writes in his essay on *Medium* that "if a person's behavior doesn't make sense to you, it's because you're missing a piece

---

2 Kalina Christoff, Alan M. Gordon, Jonathan Smallwood, Rachelle Smith, and Jonathan W. Schooler, "Experience Sampling during fMRI Reveals Default Network and Executive System Contributions to Mind Wandering," *Proceedings of the National Academy of Sciences U.S.A.* 106, no. 21 (2009): 8719–8724, doi.org/10.1073/pnas.0900234106.

3 "Survey Reveals Employee Productivity Averages 2 Hours and 53 Minutes a Day," VoucherCloud.com, January 15, 2025, vouchercloud.com/better-living/office-worker-productivity.

of their context."[4] Instead of viewing this time-frittering as a personal deficit, perhaps we should think of it as a sign that we need a break.

The context in this case could be that workers are overworked and burned out, that their brains need more downtime than they're getting. We may simply be asking for too much of their time. Coline de Silans writes in Welcome to the Jungle about Lasse Rheingans, chief executive at a German consultancy firm, who cut the workday at his company down to five hours. When he was an employee, he'd asked for two afternoons a week off to take care of his children, and quickly found that he was getting just as much done as when he'd been working full-time. Once he was running his own business, he brought that experience to the whole company. They compress their work into five hours, then take the rest of the day off.[5]

This is a sprinter's tactic, which means the essential part is that you don't fill that time with more work. During that five hours, you have to be focused and present, knowing that a break is coming. Essentially, we as humans "waste" so much time during an eight-hour day because that time is not wasted—those hours are necessary downtime. By cutting the time spent at work, we reduce the need for those breaks throughout the day.

It can feel difficult to take time away when our to-do lists grow longer and longer, but that's exactly the time that we most need to give our brains a rest. Often, we're spending our breaks still working, doing things like answering emails on our phones, multitasking. We're often trying to do entirely too many things at once. While some of these things feel like they require less of our mental energy, we still aren't letting our brains rest.

When we multitask, a cognitive bottleneck occurs, because multitasking is really multi-sequencing. Jelmer Borst, a professor

4 Devon Price, "Laziness Does Not Exist," *Medium*, March 23, 2018, humanparts.medium.com/laziness-does-not-exist-3af27e312d01.

5 Coline de Silans, "The Five-Hour Workday: Living the Dream?", February 3, 2021, welcometothejungle.com/en/articles/the-5-hour-workday-living-the-dream.

of computational cognitive neuroscience, explains in his article in the Journal of Experimental Psychology that tasks are performed in short sequences, and more tasks shorten those sequences. If each task requires what he calls a "problem state" to be maintained, even for a few seconds, then the tasks interfere with each other.[6] Your performance gets worse, because you're effectively swapping back and forth between these tasks instead of giving any of them your full attention. The more we plow through work in spite of our mental fatigue, the faster we're depleting our own batteries. We need to recharge.

Rest is essential. We often think that giving up sleep to hustle is virtuous, but skipping sleep can mess up your short- and long-term memory formation, decision-making, attention, and coordination. Many organizations, from the Cleveland Clinic to the American Heart Association, qualify chronic sleep deprivation as getting less than the recommended minimum of seven hours of sleep per night. Sleeping less than seven hours a night is a pretty regular schedule for some of us.

Your brain needs time to be off the clock, yet waking up at the crack of dawn is seen as a desirable trait. TikTok influencers, like startup founders before them, are sharing their elaborate morning routines. There was a recent trend, the "5–9 before my 9–5," where they would show their long workouts, complicated breakfasts and supplements, journaling sessions, meditation, and seven-part skin care regimens. They attribute their success to these routines, to their morning discipline.

As we've attached a morality to work, we've also attributed morality to being awake early in the morning, and are pretty judgemental of those with different schedules. But waking up at 5am is morally neutral. You are not a better person because you're an early riser and not a night owl—you're simply a person. Really, if you're

6 Jelmer P. Borst, Niels A. Taatgen, and Hedderik van Rijn, "The Problem State: a Cognitive Bottleneck in Multitasking," *Journal of Experimental Psychology. Learning, Memory, and Cognition* 36, no. 2 (2010): 363–82, doi:10.1037/a0018106.

aiming to be that ideal worker, you're basically expected to be both anyway.

Hustle culture tells you that there's no time for sleep, and we often brag about how little we're getting in the service of chasing our work goals. We weigh the importance of sleep against our other priorities, and work always comes first. And this is problematic. While there is still a lot of mystery surrounding why we sleep, scientifically speaking, one thing science does agree on is that your brain needs it.

The way that our work is structured often actively makes our sleep worse. Work schedules can be inconsistent, which makes our sleep inconsistent and uncertain. Swing shifts, "clopening" shifts (where a worker closes late in the evening only to also open early in the morning), and a schedule that changes week to week means a disruption in sleep rhythms. Jonathan White, a professor of politics at the London School of Economics and Political Science, calls these obstacles to decent sleep a political injustice. He reports that Uber drivers will sometimes sleep in their cars, because the app favors those drivers who rack up lots of hours, and that this practice leads to short and poor sleep and concerns about both privacy and safety.[7] The right to a good night's sleep isn't equally distributed, and workers who are less privileged and exploited are getting the short end of the stick.

When I worked at a factory, they kept increasing our mandatory overtime until I was usually working fourteen-hour shifts, six days a week. Because of a chronic illness, I was never really able to fit in enough sleep at home to recover for the next day and started keeping a pillow in my car, taking naps on breaks and lunchtime.

In hustle culture, we find ourselves living at odds with the demands of our bodies. But as a friend of mine likes to say, nature bats last. When you put yourself at odds with what your body requires, it is a fight that your body will ultimately win. The consequences of getting too little sleep can be deferred, but they can't be put off forever.

7 Jonathan White, "Poor Sleep," *Aeon*, March 22, 2022, aeon.co/essays/being-underslept-and-out-of-sync-is-a-political-injustice.

Bad sleep affects our physical health, and it affects our mental health too. It makes already bad circumstances feel unbearable. It makes it harder to improve those circumstances, as people are too exhausted to seek better opportunities. This kind of fatigue impairs our ability to make decisions, and inhibits our cognitive functions.

Additionally, memory depends on sleep. So much so that when you are overworked and exhausted, you may struggle to remember details about your day. *Did I mail that letter? Have I left my coffee in the microwave again? Wait, where was I driving to?*

When we sleep and/or get rest, our brains consolidate new information and commit it to memory, rehearsing recently learned skills. Scientists at the University of Birmingham have recently found that we do a bit of that when awake but resting.[8] They put volunteers into an MRI, and had them use two different sets of joysticks. One worked the way you'd expect it to, if you pushed it left, the cursor went left. Easy. The other seemed to continuously rotate clockwise. Where once left was left, now it was up and right was down—nothing went where it seemed it should, but it did so in a consistent way. Everyone in the study rested before and after using their joysticks. The people who got a normal joystick didn't have much change in their resting state networks' activity levels from this first rest break to the second. They hadn't really learned anything new that the brain would need to work on; they'd encountered a regular joystick before. But the second group, the ones who got the trick joystick, did see a difference. Their brains kept on working while they rested the second time, committing to memory the things that they had learned. And so, the study concluded that if we don't get that rest, it actually interrupts learning.

Sleep is an essential function, but it isn't the only rest our brains need. We also need time away from active problem-solving. A design professor introduced me to the "bed, bath, and bus theory." It's the idea

8 Neil B. Albert, Edwin M. Robertson, and R. Chris Miall, "The Resting Human Brain and Motor Learning," *Current Biology* 19, no. 12 (2009): 1023–7, doi:10.1016/j.cub.2009.04.028.

that you have your best ideas when your brain is occupied by other mundane things—and you've likely experienced this phenomenon plenty of times in your life. A friend told me that he was having trouble with a programming problem, and he took some time away from it to take a walk with his dog. He wasn't thinking about the problem at all, when bam, the solution came to him. This is how the human brain operates, running background processes while you go about your life.

A 2006 study found something similar, when asking students to choose the best car out of four options. Researchers had already ranked them independently, based on some factors like size and mileage, so they had a "best" in mind. Half of the students were allowed four minutes to deliberate after they reviewed the stats, to just sit and ponder. The other half were immediately distracted from thinking about the cars at all by being asked to solve anagrams. You may assume that the first group, the group who had time to sit and really consider what they'd read, would make the better choice. But they didn't.[9] Our subconscious mind offers us solutions when we leave it alone. This only works, though, when the distraction is something simple that doesn't require too much serious concentration—bed, bath, bus.

With the right kind of distractions, we can integrate information in a more complex way than when our brains are consciously working through the same problem. Recharging your mental batteries in this way means that you're more effective when you come back after a break. I've often called a coworker over to help me with something because I'd just been staring at it for too long. I'd have probably spent less time working on that project if I'd just taken a break when I started to feel burned out. It might sound very heroic to be working sixteen-hour days, but most of that time isn't going toward work, and much of it is actively working against your own brain.

---

9 Ap Dijksterhuis, Maarten W. Bos, Loran F. Nordgren, Rick B. van Baaren, "On Making the Right Choice: The Deliberation-without-Attention Effect," *Science* 311, no. 5763 (2006): 1005–7, doi:10.1126/science.1121629.

There is great irony in the fact that I have slammed up against the hard stop my brain enforces while writing this book. I have sat in the afternoon, reading and re-reading the same sentence over and over, without really absorbing any meaning from it. Suddenly unable to piece together notes into text that would be of interest to anyone. Despite the fact that I'm literally researching and writing about why this happens, I have become angry with myself. *I was doing great three hours ago! Why has my brain gone on strike?*

Michael Taft, a writer and meditation teacher, calls this phenomenon "cerebral congestion." He says that in a normal working day, so much comes at us all at once, all day long, that our brains don't have the time to process all of it. The speed of our lives doesn't really allow us to work through this backlog of unprocessed data, and we're not getting the rest that we need after learning something new. More than half of our workday is spent receiving and managing information, according to a 2010 LexisNexis survey.[10]

Think about your workday. How much of yours is spent receiving information, via emails and phone calls and meetings, and then managing that information? How much of it is spent actually using that information to do your job? My brain is often an absolute mess—there's a lot going on in there. Katie Athony wrote a piece called "Welcome to Mom Brain" that covers all of the things taking up residence in her own brain: "There is a meter, a gauge, and a monitor for everything" and "it smells like hot electronics in here."[11] I hold in my own brain the running to-do list that I have for work, and for the house, where I saw our preschooler's shoes, bits of writing I want to pursue, what spirit week horrors are coming up, where I could find something with the Grinch on it before tomorrow, if I've drank any water today, all the lyrics to REM's "It's The End of the

---

10 The 2010 International Workplace Productivity Survey, commissioned by LexisNexis, multivu.com/players/English/46619-LexisNexis-International-Workplace-Productivity-Survey/.

11 Katie Anthony, "Welcome to Mom Brain," KatyKatiKate.com, November 8, 2017, katykatikate.com/the-blog//2017/11/welcome-to-mom-brain.html.

World as We Know It," how much milk we have left, and a haunting feeling that I am forgetting something very, very important. And as Katie helpfully points out, this is my brain. This is where I live. It's the same thing I use to write, to be creative, to think all the deep and interesting thoughts that make being a person worthwhile—all of this happens in the same brain. It is full. We need more time, to be able to slow down enough to empty it just a bit. To process all the data that lives there, so that it can perhaps stop living there.

Your cognitive resources are finite, just as your physical ones are. Hustle culture insists that more work is always better, but Anders Ericsson disagrees. Ericsson is essentially an expert on experts, studying the most successful people on Earth and how they build expertise. He finds that practice does make perfect, but only if people are practicing the right way. Experts in their field don't grind for hours on end, but work for a few hours very intentionally. In fact, he finds that regardless of their discipline, it's rare to find someone at the top of their game who averages more than four hours of practice a day.[12] This is, again, a sprinter's tactic. When you're fully and intensely focused on something, you can't sustain that level of engagement all day.

Four or five hours a day is consistently the upper limit of deliberate practice like this, and Geoff Colvin, author of several books on human achievement and world-class performers, writes that practice sessions generally only last for an hour to ninety minutes. When they don't allow for sufficient breaks and recovery, people end up with overtraining injuries and burnout. Research like Ericsson's and Colvin's show that long workdays are just not designed to get the best from people, and that they're seeing diminishing returns on their effort.

It doesn't benefit me to spend ten hours practicing the violin for the sake of saying that I spent ten hours at it. But spending an

12 Chris Weller, "Forget the 9 to 5—Research Suggests There's a Case for the 3-Hour Workday," *Business Insider*, September 26, 2017, businessinsider.com/8-hour-workday-may-be-5-hours-too-long-research-suggests-2017-9.

hour a day working intentionally on specific goals would help me to improve my playing. Whether we're programming or moving rocks, we're more effective at hour three than we are at hour fifteen, and continuing to trudge along instead of resting like we should leads us to burnout. This is one of the biggest arguments in favor of schedule changes like a four-day workweek, although some research suggests that a switch to a shorter workday (five or six hours instead of eight) would also be a smart change.

Sweden selected a group of retirement-home workers in Gothenburg to work a six-hour schedule five days a week as part of a government study. Workers were happier, less stressed, and enjoyed their work more. Dave Rhoads, founder of Blue Street Capital, an equipment financing firm, moved his company to a five-hour workday ten years ago, and reports that their revenue is up 150% since the change.

Research shows us that we can only focus in shorter bursts, that we need downtime to process all the information that comes at us, and that our brain solves problems when we are away from our work, and that all seems to suggest that we should be spending less hours actively working and more time resting and recovering. Tellingly, none of the research seems to show that we should be working *more.*

In short, downtime makes us better workers. Work takes up huge chunks of our brain space, and we don't allow enough time to process and analyze all of this information. It may seem counterintuitive, but idleness, and the space and quiet that it provides us, is essential to getting work done. Downtime replenishes our stores of attention and motivation, and is needed in every part of our lives from encouraging creativity and innovation to simply forming stable memories. We need it to work effectively.

But more importantly, downtime makes us human. Our brains never truly stop. In the 1990s, Marcus Raichle and his team discovered that the brain constantly uses around 20% of all your body's energy, and it uses a little more when you're doing something that requires a lot of concentration. Spotting those areas that light up with great concentration also helped them to find the areas that don't, and it turns out those inactive parts all fire up together when you are resting and letting your mind wander. Those inactive parts were named the default mode network (DMN), and it's not the only resting-state network in our brains. But it's the one that is responsible for our ability to understand how humans behave, build a code of ethics, and even form our own identities.[13] We literally need this downtime to be human. It allows our brains to make sense of things we've learned, and to resolve problems in our lives.

When our mind wanders, we replay conversations we've had, and work through our to-do lists, and we think about our lives and our place in the world. We seek solutions, we revisit experiences, and we form our sense of self. Hustle culture asks that we work in a way that's contrary to the way our brains function, and in ways that ultimately make us less whole as humans.

It Causes Burnout

Hustle culture is burnout culture. It's not possible to live up to the standards of being an ideal worker, dedicating our entire selves only to work, without eventually getting burned out.

The idea that the pace of modern life would run us down is one with plenty of historical precedent. Anne Helen Petersen's article "How Millennials Became the Burnout Generation," which later evolved into her book *Can't Even,* notes that burnout was first recognized as a psychological diagnosis in 1974, by Herbert Freudenberger. But the feeling existed long before then.

In the book of Ecclesiastes, it was called "melancholic world weariness." It was called neurasthenia, or nervous exhaustion in the late 1800s, and Josh Cohen, a psychoanalyst who specializes in burnout, notes in his article in the *Economist* that it was endemic to the

13 Ferris Jabr, "Why Your Brain Needs More Downtime," *Scientific American,* October 15, 2013, scientificamerican.com/article/mental-downtime/.

renaissance. Cohen defines burnout as having no internal resources left, yet being compelled to just keep on working anyway. We are, as a people, overwhelmed and out of internal resources. We have so many pings for our attention that we become less likely to respond to any of them; instead we become overstimulated and shut down. These feelings can bleed out into the rest of our lives, not only our work, so that we feel just as overwhelmed and detached in our downtime.

Melancholia, neurasthenia, sickness of the soul, burnout. This idea that the very culture we live in is the cause of our suffering goes back centuries, yet we don't always recognize when it's happening. In order to fight against burnout, we have to fight against hustle culture.

Burnout may sound like a buzzword used to sell lavender candles and yoga retreats, but it's more than just feeling tired of work. Exhaustion is the aspect of burnout that we talk about the most, in part because it is such a badge of honor in our culture. But Christina Maslach and Michael Leiter, two psychologists who quite literally wrote the book on burnout, invented something called the Burnout Inventory. This assessment grades the level of burnout someone is suffering on three key profiles: exhaustion, cynicism, and perception of effectiveness.[14] The assessment of these three profiles looks at how we hold up the ideals that we have for work—up against our reality.

Perhaps we expected to be fighting poverty, teaching, or healing, but most of our day is paperwork and administrative burdens. If we give up our ideals, we become cynical. People want their work to mean something, to have some significance. Feeling like you're just ticking boxes can quickly lead to total disengagement.

But if we ignore that reality, and hold tight to our idealism, we end up feeling ineffective and frustrated, like our work doesn't matter. Frustrated workers can have a hard time seeing the good that they

---

14 Christina Maslach and Susan E. Jackson, "The Measurement of Experienced Burnout," *Journal of Organizational Behavior* 2: (1981), 99–113, doi.org/10.1002/job.4030020205.

are accomplishing, especially in service work, where it's harder to see an abstract outcome. This is why the common advice when you're feeling helpless is to make something, literally anything, because then it's easy to see your accomplishment. You grew a plant, you knitted a sock, you made a table—it's physically right in front of you. Helping someone is much more abstract.

There is a third option, to hold tight to both our reality and our ideals. When we try to square the two, we become exhausted, as we're constantly pulled between them.

Exhaustion, cynicism, ineffectiveness—the trifecta of burnout. Yet most conversations about burnout only touch on exhaustion, because hustle culture valorizes it. It's much harder to brag about being jaded or ineffective or frustrated, and so we don't even really talk about those aspects, making it harder for us to recognize our burnout.

The mismatch between a worker's ideals and their reality doesn't always come from the work itself. As Jonathan Malesic points out in his book, *The End of Burnout*, we may find great fulfillment in the actual work that we're doing, but become burned out because of other parameters of our jobs. People may find a mismatch in the control they have (or don't have) over their schedule, in fairness around promotions, or in not feeling the sense of community they'd hoped to.

Most of us are pulled between the expectations of our work and the reality of it. Still, we don't see it. We fall into the trap of thinking that our work simply isn't the kind of thing that causes burnout. *That's for aid workers or high-powered lawyers. People with more difficult or stressful sorts of jobs.* We assume that since we're still managing, still getting work done, that we must not be burned out. We still feel like we're accomplishing *something*, after all. We're not *that* cynical. We're okay.

But are we? Recognizing lower-level stakes, catching burnout when it starts, could mean treating the problem before it gets worse.

So often, we just don't see it until we're already exhausted and fully disengaged.

While we are much more able to recognize when we're pushing too far physically than when we're pushing too far mentally, both can lead to catastrophic results. Brianna Sacks, an ultramarathon runner, wrote about her own experience with overtraining syndrome, describing how her body had gone haywire on nearly every front. Even as her condition kept worsening, she felt that she had to keep going.

There was so much to do. She had scheduled races to train for, assignments for her job as a reporter, and a full social life. She had put her body through a great amount of stress without giving it enough rest, hustling as most of us feel compelled to do. Unlike most of us, she ran ultramarathons as a hobby and had upped her training to running seventy to eighty miles a week when she realized she had finally overdone it. That she'd so stressed and overtrained her body that it simply stopped working.

When she finally relented and went to the doctor, he told her that her cortisol levels were off the chart, a telltale sign that your body has been pushed too far. At this point, your body actually tries to protect itself by shutting down, and if you continue to ignore those warning signs, it starts to harm your organs.

Overtraining syndrome isn't all that well understood, but it seems to happen when athletes fail to recover in the way that they need to. Their immune and parasympathetic nervous systems stop working correctly. Most athletic training focuses on functional overreach, where you push your body to do a little more than it can, followed by a rest period that induces adaptations. Think of the gradual overload of a weight lifting program, where you increase the weight just a bit every time.

But this can easily turn into non-functional overreach. An athlete will push themselves, but instead of resting afterward, they push themselves even more. Instead of adapting, this kind of overreach causes damage to your body. The training is the same either way—the only difference between adaptation and damage is the amount of rest. The body breaks down instead of rebuilding stronger.

If you think this would never be a problem for you, because you can't think of a single thing on this Earth that you'd like to do less than train for an ultramarathon, the same kind of damage can be caused by overwork. Your body doesn't know, or care, where stress is coming from. Whether it's work stress, physical stress, or emotional stress. Stress is stress, and it affects our bodies negatively.

As Micah Ling writes in her Outside Online article on physical burnout, pushing through for too long is a physiological stressor, and it requires a big response from your immune system to restore it. It pulls energy from your other systems to make up the difference, dipping into your hormonal, cognitive, and metabolic functions. It pumps out cortisol to help your body endure it. But if you're always pumping out cortisol, your body will actually start to make less of it, and stress becomes harder to deal with.[15] By overtraining, people who were once able to run hard for twenty-four hours in ultramarathons damage their bodies so badly they can barely walk around the block. Their bodies can no longer tolerate the stress they're used to subjecting it to.

For many suffering from this syndrome, like those with chronic illnesses and disabilities, their body is never the same. Burnout, whether mental or physical, can damage your life in very real, very big ways. Hustle culture tells us to keep going, to keep doing, damn the costs. But this is a recipe for stress and damage.

You cannot sprint through the ultramarathon that is your life. Our ideals can't be squared with our realities, because hustle culture's demands are unrealistic. Putting work above everything else in your

---

15 Micah Ling, "Why Burnout Is More Complicated than You Think," *Trail Runner Magazine*, OutsideOnline.com, June 29, 2023, outsideonline.com/health/running/training-advice/recovery/burnout-is-complicated/.

life is, very simply, not good for you. Pushing through and ignoring every signal your body gives you is also not good for you. But this is what hustle culture demands of us, and we are so fully immersed in it that it can be hard for us to see how it's affecting us.

Fighting burnout means rejecting hustle culture and its demands. Developing a strong sense of boundaries around giving our body what it needs, reframing what success means for us individually, and resisting the urge to hustle. We have to build lives that are sustainable, and that can look different for each of us.

It Devalues People

There are problems with hustle culture beyond burnout. A system that only attaches worth to work, and really only to work that garners a wage, devalues humans of all kinds. It devalues the very young and the very old. It devalues the people who care for them. It devalues the sick and the disabled.

There are people among us who are unable to do anything that our culture would qualify as productive. They can't hold a regular job, they aren't caring for children, they aren't able to clean their homes or cook their meals. Would you say that these people aren't valuable? Would you say it to their face?

We are all closer to disability than we think, yet our culture talks about those who aren't able to participate in capitalism as nothing but a drain. But every human matters, and every one of us has dignity, regardless of our ability to work. Still, hustle culture doesn't value all of us and can be actively bad for our health.

I know a bit about this on a personal level. Medically, I am a lemon. I came down with Lyme disease in my teens, but doctors weren't able to figure out why I was so sick for another six years. I didn't know why I felt so badly either, and I thought I could just power through it. The culture that I've grown up in said that I should just keep pushing, so I did. Since every doctor said that my labs looked normal, I figured everyone else must feel like garbage too, and they managed to work and have social lives anyway. I decided that I would hustle, like they did. I finished an accelerated graduate school program, worked long hours at a full-time job, started my own business, and photographed twenty weddings in one year, while working said full-time job. I also managed to get mono somehow, spent any time that I wasn't working barely able to move, and got so sick that I slept for twenty-two hours straight. I spent several years getting PICC lines put in so that I could give myself IV antibiotics at home. The delay in diagnosing my Lyme turned it into A Whole Thing, and I have since acquired more chronic health issues like horrible little Pokémons.

This kind of illness and disability consistently takes time away from people, but work is still usually the last thing that we'll let go.

Because our culture says that we're only valuable when we're producing money, though, I went to great lengths to keep working. There was a point where all of my time at home was spent resting enough that I could go back to work the next day. I couldn't really focus on my health the way that I needed to, so I was kind of slapping a bandaid on my illness so that I could shamble through another Tuesday.

Getting through the workweek would have been easier for me if I'd been able to work less hours, or with a more flexible schedule, or even if I'd just let the people in my office know what was going on with me. The way that I was expected to work—to be fully committed to the job, to work any amount of hours, to do whatever it takes—wasn't something that I had the ability to do. I still don't. Those who are disabled or are caregivers (and many of us fall into both categories) have other hard demands on our time.

Disabled people may find it difficult-to-impossible to participate in the kinds of workplaces that embrace the hustle. Every chronic illness has its own limitations and needs, and they change inconveniently often. Many of us have to be more protective of our sleep. For able-bodied people, pulling an all-nighter might mean needing some extra coffee the next day. For people with certain illnesses, it could mean a seizure. Hustling isn't great for anyone's health, but it's spectacularly bad for anyone with a chronic health problem. Because of the limitations our brains and bodies put on us, we may have fewer hours in a day that we're able to be productive. Those workable hours are whittled down even further by treatments, doctor's appointments, and tests.

When you are disabled, or chronically ill, it's important to set healthy boundaries around your work, but this can be difficult to do. It means figuring out the accommodations you might need, and how best to ask for them. It means considering if you'll need an outside agency's help. Often, it's hard to even talk about these concerns with your workplace, because you may be uncomfortable talking about your health or unable to answer their questions. *I don't know when I'll be back, I don't know if I'll be back, I don't know if I'll be okay.*

It's understandable that you'd be worried your job may penalize you for being sick. While it's still illegal to fire someone because of this, there's plenty of cover for them to say they aren't promoting you for other reasons. It's easy to feel like maybe it would be better to just keep it to yourself, and I've done that at a number of jobs. I wore long sleeves even in the summer, so that the PICC line I needed wouldn't show. I found ways to cope with continuing to send my little emails when I was in an enormous amount of pain. I went to the emergency room after my shift was over more times than was really reasonable. It's difficult to share something that feels private with your supervisor, and there is always the fear that you're giving up what little job security you have.

Even Christina Applegate, who has some of the privileges that being a famous actress can afford you, found it difficult to speak up at work and set the boundaries that she needed to get through a workday. She described in her 2023 interview with *Vanity Fair* how she still had to deal with network execs who were not sympathetic, and people who simply don't understand all the ways that her MS makes doing her job harder.

Hiding chronic health problems is incredibly stressful, which is really bad for your health. But hustle culture tells us that we must put work above all else, even our health. This was glaringly obvious during the pandemic, when corporations wanted the economy back up and running, even if people died because of it.

If you're able-bodied, you may feel like none of this will ever be relevant to you. But we are all a car accident, an autoimmune disease, a viral pandemic, or a few decades of aging away from disability. Getting sick with a simple virus like EBV or Covid, even the flu, can lead to disability down the road, and Americans spend more years sick than the rest of the world. Part of the reason is that we're living for more years. In 2000, people in America lived with an illness for 10.9 years on average, and our life expectancy was around 76 years.[16] That's around 14% of our lives spent dealing with illness. Currently, our average life expectancy is 79 years, and we spend 12.4 years of that time sick on average, which is around 16% of our lives.[17] Even adjusted for the increase in life expectancy, we are spending more of our time in worse health. This gap, between our life span and our health in those years, is widening around the world, as chronic illnesses take up larger chunks of people's lives.

Unfortunately, there's a pervasive belief that chronic illness is a punishment for something done wrong. That a person must be sick because they didn't exercise enough, or they ate poorly, or they ignored their doctor's advice, or they didn't lead decent lives. Some people want to believe this because it helps them to believe that illness and disability will never happen to them. If it's just a matter of getting exercise, then they will simply do that, and they'll never have to worry about being sick. But the truth is that humans fall victim to entropy. We just get sick, through no fault of our own. It isn't

---

16 "U.S. Life Expectancy (1950–2025)," MacroTrends, n.d., macrotrends.net/global-metrics/countries/USA/united-states/life-expectancy.

17 Amber Tong, "Americans Spend More Years Sick Than the Rest of the World," *Bloomberg*, December 11, 2024, bloomberg.com/news/articles/2024-12-11/americans-spend-more-years-sick-than-rest-of-the-world-new-study-show.

a predicament that you can exercise, or pray, or work your way out of. So we should treat every person with dignity, whether they are working or not, because these things could happen to any one of us.

The idea that people who are disabled are still able to find meaning in their lives is actually threatening to our whole hustle culture value system. If we attach our worth to work, and someone isn't working, well, how dare they view themself as worthy?

But to write that out, in black and white, seems bonkers. That I would even have to type out a sentence declaring that humans are worthy and valuable, even if they are not earning money is offensive. Disabled people have done great things for the world. They've created mutual aid groups and rallied for their political demands. They form priceless relationships with their friends and family. Their very lives show us that there are more important things in this world than whether or not you have a paid job. And many of them are working, and doing very important work at that, but they aren't doing it in a way that capitalism values.

But what if our culture did value it? It could justify better working conditions, legitimize unpaid care work as valuable, and even support systems like universal basic income (UBI).

In *Work Won't Love You Back*, Sarah Jaffe writes about Loretta Domencich, an organizer with Milwaukee's Welfare Rights Organization, who has compared UBI to the way that their tribe did things before the natives were colonized, where every person was valued regardless of what they were able to do. They made sure that everyone in their community was cared for.[18] The idea that every person is deserving of dignity can liberate not only the disabled from the guilt of "not working," it can liberate us all.

18 Sarah Jaffe, *Work Won't Love You Back: How Devotion to Our Jobs Keeps Us Exploited, Exhausted, and Alone* (Bold Type Books, 2022).

It Devalues Care Work

Hustle culture is also untenable for caregivers. In the same way that you can't put off a chemo treatment or a health crisis, you can't just put off a child who needs to be fed or a sick parent because of work. Caregiving makes the entire world function, and almost every single one of us will have to take care of someone else—it isn't just parents. A 2020 report from the AARP said that nearly 30 million Americans had cared for an ill friend or family member while working a paid job, which is about a 5 million increase from 2015.

Our economy, our workplaces, even our civil defense requires care work. Hustle culture would have you believe that you should still, somehow, be working those long hours regardless of your other responsibilities. If you aren't, you must not be all that ambitious. But as a caregiver, there are obligations on your time outside of work, and all the hours in a day are not yours. You are simply not able to prioritize work over everything else when you have a child or are caring for a parent or spouse.

Caregiving burnout happens in the same way that workplace burnout does. Expectations for what makes a good parent have only expanded, and busyness as a parent is as much a badge of pride as it is at work. We show our status by showing how positively overworked and frenzied and hectic and *busy* we are.

Moms are supposed to be making it look effortless and joyful. But if you make it look effortless, then it doesn't look like work, and of course we must be working. So you have to clarify to everyone around you how much you actually are working, but it's not really work, because you love it, but also it is. Like overwork, we equate our exhaustion at our caregiving responsibilities with devotion. There is not enough time in the day to do all the things we want to do to be good parents, and yet we try.

Caregivers are a rock for those living with illness and disability, and it's so often a full-time job. We give until we break. If the system is rigged against us, our inclination is to just try harder. If we're working all day, and caring for someone all night, and thus have no time at all for ourselves, we often end up just sleeping less. But if we're already barely able to function through a full day of work, because disability or illness is sucking the life out of us, we're actually going to have to sleep more, so we'll be giving up that downtime for ourselves.

The answer is never less work.

Malandra Hastick created The Wellness Sauce, an online community that focuses on wellness habits, and she actually defines *burnout* in a context that does not directly involve work, as "the inability to sustain your wellness"; for a person to heal from their burnout, from regular work or care work, the circumstances around them have to change.[19] Hassle Aviles, executive director of Not 9 to 5, a non-profit that advocates for better mental health in hospitality and tourism workplaces, says in a 2022 *Bustle* article that one of the biggest differences between burnout and regular exhaustion is that burnout is associated with a lack of support.[20] This is why you can resolve regular exhaustion with rest, but burnout requires real change to your environment. Caregivers of all kinds lack real structural support. The root cause of burnout is a system that views us all as disposable.

Every politician who votes down paid leave, universal childcare, or universal basic income is saying that the market simply has a right to free care work, writes Meg Conley in a 2022 *Harper's Bazaar* article about the Great Resignation.[21] Our society has decided that figuring out what to do with your children while you work is your problem, individually. Yet the world cannot turn without care work. We can't

19 Eve Ettinger, "Have We Been Thinking About Burnout All Wrong?", *Bustle*, March 7, 2022, bustle.com/wellness/burnout-definition-what-we-get-wrong.

20 Ibid

21 Meg Conley, "What the Conversation around 'The Great Resignation' Leaves Out," *Harper's Bazaar*, January 31, 2022, harpersbazaar.com/culture/features/a38941844/what-the-conversation-around-the-great-resignation-leaves-out/.

have a functioning economic system without schools and childcare. Someone has to watch the kids, but we've created a system where most of us can't afford to do it ourselves, so we underpay care workers to do it for us while we earn money elsewhere, or we put it on our family to do the work for free. And that care work is valuable work. Researchers say that if we actually added all care work to the GDP, it would increase by more than four trillion dollars.

For example, we built a photography studio recently, and it required a lot of our time. I asked my dad to foreman the project, because he knows how to wire electrical outlets, hang drywall, and build rooms that won't collapse, and I don't. I asked my husband to help out, because he's got me beat on upper body strength by a wide margin. I am endlessly grateful to both of them, and could not have possibly finished the project without them. I am also endlessly grateful to my mother, and could not have possibly finished the project without her. She didn't staple in insulation or drill holes for cables, but she watched our children so that my husband and I could both work. If she hadn't, I wouldn't have been able to do it. Because someone has to care for the children. I cannot do my work if my kids aren't safe.

Care work isn't only necessary for other paid labor; it's also an essential part of civil defense and activism. Who's doing the dishes—or making dinner, teaching kids, cleaning the house, or staffing a precinct for voters—while people are planning a protest for better labor rights?

Care work is at the base of all the other work that we do. Yet it still feels like a revolutionary act to mention the people who are doing the work. Melanie Lynskey thanked her nanny in an acceptance speech, and it makes all the sense in the world to me. How could I focus on my work without knowing my kids are cared for? That they're somewhere they're safe and happy? She certainly can't have her kids run around on set unsupervised. If your parent has dementia, you can't just leave them home alone to fend for themselves while you go to the office. We simply cannot work without caregivers, and yet we constantly overlook it as work that is important, and we set up our work schedules in a way that makes it incredibly difficult to navigate.

When a parent can't bend their work schedule to accommodate their kids, they have to pay someone else to do it. And it's very, very expensive. In America, the average cost for childcare is about $11,400 per year. We currently have one child in preschool and one in elementary school. This gives me between the hours of 9:00am and 3:20pm to work—less, if it requires a commute of any kind. That is not a full-time work schedule, and few good jobs (the kind that offer benefits and maybe have some potential for advancement) make room for part-time workers.

While school is most workers' primary source of childcare, it only runs for nine months of the year and maybe two-thirds of a workday. These schedules simply do not line up. And if you want any assistance, any access to social safety nets, you have to work. To receive SNAP benefits in Pennsylvania, you have to work an average of twenty hours a week.[22] It's a bit more complicated than that, because it's a government program, but that is the gist.

But parents *are* working, and welfare rights groups have argued that the work they're doing deserves support. Wages for Housework has argued that capitalism requires this work done in the home, because it produces new workers, and that makes it worthy of being paid. Demanding pay was a way for them to point out that this work is real work, of real importance. Nancy Folbre, an economist, once wrote that two single mothers could simply swap kids for eight hours a day, and earn more than $10,000 a year in babysitting services for work that they were going to do anyway for their own kids.[23]

The demand for care work right now is bigger than the supply, and the best solution seems to be more common utility (services or resources that we are all able to use, like streetlights or libraries).

---

22 Supplemental Nutrition Assistance Program (SNAP) Work Requirements, pa.gov/en/agencies/dhs/resources/snap/snap-work-requirements-abawds.html.

23 Jaffe, *Work Won't Love You Back.*

There's an economic theory, called the tragedy of the commons, that asserts that this solution will never work. That any common resources can't be managed fairly, and will be used up inefficiently.

It turns out, though, that this theory isn't true. Elinor Ostrom even won the Nobel Prize in economics for proving that it isn't true. She showed that communities have always managed common resources in a sustainable way, that things don't need to be privatized to be protected. Universal paid leave would give parents the choice to care for their babies, and universal child care would mean that they could do other work. Universal basic income would offer more security to all of us.

When we can't live up to the expectations of our culture, we blame ourselves, but it's a shared societal problem. We subsidize farmers and bail out car makers, and our K-12 education is free. But we can't get subsidized care, because we don't value domestic labor; the market feels entitled to it.

Hustle culture needs us caregivers, but it certainly hopes that we don't notice that.

Chapter 2: How Did We Get Here? A History of Hustle Culture

So this devotion to overwork goes against the way our brains operate, it burns us out, and it doesn't value us. How did work get like this?

Long ago, people labored to meet their materials needs. We needed food, water, and shelter, and acquiring those things was a large percentage of the work that we were doing. There were no emails or spreadsheets, but the biggest difference is that we weren't working to make money for someone else. There was no putting in extra hours to impress the boss so that you'd get a promotion down the line; you grew a carrot so that you could eat a carrot. Then, Ferdinand Magellan circumnavigated the globe.

As Joyce Appleby explains in her book about the history of capitalism, trade flourished after that, and new kinds of work arose, like processing all the goods that came in from these expeditions. That was a type of job that simply hadn't existed before; there wasn't a need for it. While trade routes were being established, we were also finding more effective ways to raise food, which means that workers were also free to do new and different kinds of work.[24] The workers then became separated from the tools and farm plots that once gave them their independence, and they no longer had the resources needed to meet their material needs on their own. Instead of selling their goods, they sold their labor.

24 Joyce Appleby, *The Relentless Revolution: A History of Capitalism* (W.W. Norton & Company, 2011).

I skipped a few things, but anyway, that's why we have capitalism now.

Capitalism seems, in retrospect, inevitable. But working only to support our own community was the norm for thousands of years. And it didn't change because it was just human nature to suddenly want money, or common sense that we would sell our labor to someone else. Historical developments, truly dramatic changes, were required to change people's habits and the way that they viewed work.

People don't inherently desire money. They want to live in a certain way, to have the things that the money will afford them. Money doesn't have any intrinsic value on its own, the way that gold or a pig or a house does. Money has the value that we confer on it, and a cultural change was necessary for us to see it as something of value.

Max Weber, a central figure in the development of sociology as a field, noted that an interesting convergence was happening in these economically advanced countries, that Protestantism arose there and brought with it the spirit of capitalism. The Protestants believed that prosperity was evidence of God's favor. If you're doing well financially, it is because you are good. Labor was virtuous in itself. Capitalism is an economic system, but it's also a cultural one. This change in people's mindset about the way that they should work, and in their morals around prosperity and labor, is a crucial part of capitalism.

Just like the explosion of remote work and the technologies that support it changed our work expectations drastically, the same was true after the second industrial revolution, when factory owners discovered that every hour could be a workable hour. Factory owners were reluctant to leave the machines idle when someone could be working them, so it was common for a workday to be fourteen or sixteen hours long, every day but Sunday. Time was money. Appleby tells us that this industrialization came quickly in England, and that capitalism overtook the way things used to be done inside of 150 years.[25] Which, on the timeline of human history, is like a weekend.

Dividing labor may have led to us selling our time, but it isn't without benefits. It allowed people to specialize, so doctors could focus on learning how to amputate a leg without also having to grow all of their own food or build their house. Personally, I am a terrible gardener, and would starve if I were responsible for growing or hunting everything that I eat, but I have other skills that are useful. Productivity increases when you're focusing on just one job, so dividing labor also means that more could be done by the same people in the same amount of time. It makes us more efficient.

But as Karl Marx rather famously argued, there's a coercion that's inherent to free enterprise. You can say that people are free to take a job or not, and that's true. But they aren't free from a need to work if they want food or shelter, or healthcare, or property. You can go off the grid and take up homesteading, but if you need to see a doctor, then you need money. If you want to build a homestead, then you need to buy land. When you don't already own the things to produce what you need, then you become beholden to an employer.

Historically, labor unions fought for those employers to treat you fairly. After WWI, our labor unions were powerful, bargaining together for high wages, worker safety, protected time off, and generous benefits. Bosses would try to take some of our money or benefits back, and workers would strike to keep them. Our grandfathers talk about getting good jobs in the coal mines and steel mills—what industries are considered to be good jobs now?

We've convinced workers that terrible conditions are normal, that we shouldn't expect fair hours or a living wage, or even to be treated like a person. This is how things work in America, and rebelling against it just shows how entitled our generation supposedly is. Overwork and constant surveillance, stress, instability—this is just the way the world is. We've lost our empathy for organized labor, and

25 Appleby, *Relentless Revolution.*

the public has stopped seeing unions as good for the economy, for jobs. But labor is all of us. Labor is people.

We have to be willing to fight again for everyone's futures. It's important to remember this, because our culture has become so focused on individualization. *Your life is your own problem. You've made your choices, and you had the freedom to choose, so we have no reason to even sympathize with you, let alone help you.*

But we are truly all in this together, and pulling yourself up by your bootstraps is not only physically impossible, it's not enough to improve your working conditions.

None of this is inevitable. Remembering that is important because if we want to really think about the choices that we have, and to make good policy decisions and agitate for change, it hurts us to talk about capitalism like it's a predetermined chapter of history. Something that simply happened to us, and not a thing that humans created, the result of many dramatic developments. It means that we currently view capitalism, and the hustle culture that developed around it, as though it's unchangeable. To make positive changes, we need to believe that change is possible.

We Do This to Ourselves

Capitalism was not inevitable, and neither was hustle culture. Our work culture is one that we've collectively cultivated, that runs on this belief—that the only way to be valued is to pour more and more hours into our work.

Much of this is driven by forces outside our personal control. There are big, systemic reasons that we work entirely too much. The consultant class moving into leadership roles across different industries meant that they brought their ideas about what makes a good worker with them. The rise of the gig economy and corporations shifting ever more risk from themselves to their workers, and companies increasing their surveillance of workers, leave us with little job security and a need to prove our work. And our moral framework doesn't allow for the idea that work is morally neutral. All of these things contribute to a culture that valorizes overwork.

But for many of us, especially creatives, the call is coming from inside the house. Hustle culture convinces us to do this to ourselves. We bought the hustle. There are certain types of work that we romanticize, and the long hours that they supposedly require along with them, until overwork becomes something that we impose on ourselves. We work without pay, we skip lunches, we miss family obligations, and we forego sleep to do more of this glorious work. This has worked so well in some industries that now the idea of working for your passion has seeped into every kind of work. Hustle culture tells us that this is good. Working is virtuous, and so working more must be even more virtuous.

It's hard to resist the culture that you're immersed in, and over time, you start to buy into the hustle and grind mindset. You already look like the bad guy if you're not interested in working overtime every day. Soon enough, you're working on that project in your free time at home. You're posting "rise n' grind" to your socials, bragging about your late nights and long weekends cranking out work. You see influencers posting their schedules, where they get up at 3 or 4 in the morning to meditate, or free write, or go to the gym, or eat one solitary poached egg in total silence. They look successful, so they must be on the right track.

You wake up at 3am now too. You work so hard to assure yourself and everyone else of your worth, but there's never enough assurance. You're only as good as your next big win, so you can't ever really work hard enough. You talk about working for the passion, the love, not the money. Which is just as well, since you aren't being paid much. Now, you scoff at people who leave their work at work, and aren't willing to fill every second of their lives with it. They're not passionate innovators, like you are. They're not hungry. They don't love the work, like you do.

This is the culture we've built. We are always, always working, and we're so proud of it. Our ability to never stop working is a badge of honor, no matter what it costs us. This is hustle culture, work above all else. When someone asks how we're doing, we say, "Busy!"—because our culture has no social taboo to saying you're overextended and overworked. The only taboo is in opting out of it.

We Want Meaning

It's so easy for us to succumb to hustle culture because we want meaning in our work. As our work has changed, our reasons for working have changed as well. Your workday may have once consisted of chopping wood so that you could build a fire and have heat. There was a very direct line from your labor to what you got from it. I chopped wood, and look, now I have a fire. These days, we hit a button and our houses get warmer, and we don't have to spend the day chopping firewood.

I'm glad for this advancement, and I don't want to go back to a time where I had to build a fire before I could have a cup of coffee. But it has changed the way that we work. We work for more than just a material good, and many of us work for more than just money. We've come to expect growth and a sense of purpose from our careers; we may even love what we do. But loving your work doesn't make the labor behind it disappear, and it doesn't mean that you want your work to be your whole life.

Hustle culture persists in part because we fear losing work that we find meaningful. But hustle culture is, really, burnout culture. We burn ourselves out because we believe that work is the path to fulfillment. When you view your job as just a paycheck, it's easier to clock out at the end of a workday, because that's the contract we've made. I show up, I get paid, and I leave my work at work. But when the work you're doing is meaningful to you, you have a different relationship to it. It's not "just" a job anymore. We've come to expect meaning from our work, but our expectations don't always line up with our reality.

There is a line between what we think should be done for love, and what we think should be done for money. But if you want to allow people the time to do something for love, then they need to be paid for it.

I'll admit that when I learned that a friend was being paid to take care of her sick wife, through a home care program, I thought that it was weird that someone would accept money for that. *Shouldn't you care for a loved one out of the goodness of your heart? They wouldn't have to pay me to care for my sick spouse, I would want to do it.*

But if she were home caring for her wife, for no pay, where would the money come from? How would they continue to buy food and pay their medical bills? If she weren't paid for her care work, she'd have to get a job elsewhere, and that would make it impossible to do the care work.

It's an argument I made in my last book, *Punk Rock Entrepreneur*, about the idea of bands selling out and getting paid to make music. If they aren't making money, they have to get another job. That means significantly less time to produce music and tour. If you love an artist and want them to keep being able to make their art, then you should pay them. We romanticize artists and the things they create, but then aren't willing to make material changes that would help them carry on creating them.

When I went to college for graphic design, there was always a debate about whether it could ever be considered a fine art or if, by its very definition, it must be commercial art. To the fine artists, this was a very important distinction, as fine art has been seen historically as something that is opposed to capital. *We do not make art for something so vulgar as money.* Lewis Hyde even argued that because artists were gifted with their talents, it only makes sense that they would give away that art to the world.[26]

---

26 Lewis Hyde, *The Gift: Creativity and the Artist in the Modern World, 25th anniversary ed.* (Vintage, 2009), 186–189.

The drive to make something just because we love to do it is a fundamental part of the human experience. But just because people still manage to make beauty in the world under terrible regimes, dealing with poverty and oppression, doesn't make that an ideal world. How many great works have we missed out on because artists simply didn't have the resources they needed? As more people are feeling squeezed from all sides, taking on second jobs and extra gigs, it's becoming harder to find the time to create. Wages stagnate, but the cost of rent has gone up, and that bohemian artist lifestyle isn't as possible as it once was. If we want to live in a world where people create wonderful things, we have to find a way that allows those people to survive, and thrive. *Creative* was once a term that could only be applied to God himself. Later, we began applying it to mere mortals, but it maintained a sense that creativity was a work of imagination, not production. Art was not—could not be—labor.

And yet, here we are, existing under capitalism, and art is labor. Art has, in fact, always been labor. This labor, and the money received for it, doesn't negate the art. Jan van Eyck didn't wake up feeling suddenly inspired to paint the richest guy in town and his many jewels, that man paid van Eyck to paint his portrait. The Sistine Chapel was painted on commission. During the Renaissance, wealthy people invested in art, and hired the best artist they could afford to paint themselves, their families, and their stuff. Artists had patrons, so that they could afford to eat and live and buy paint. Of course, these artists also probably loved to paint. They were wildly talented at it, and I imagine may have even seen their work as part of their identity. But I have a hard time imagining them guiltily taking less payment because they enjoyed producing it. It was art, and it was love, and it was also a job.

When mass production became possible, the artist was seen as something different from craftsmen working in factories. Art was valued because, get this, it was not produced by machines. An oil painting was worth whatever you paid for it, because not just anyone could get it. You could only get an oil painting from a real life artist. While AI threatens to steal our creative opportunities, it's more important than ever to understand that art is labor. That your love can also be your livelihood. There are companies who view computer-generated works as "good enough," diminishing real art, while also taking very real wages away from workers. It can make every job in the creative industry feel like it might be the last we get, feeding the hustle machine.

The biggest offender, perhaps, is spec work. Spec work is done on speculation, for free, often in the form of a contest. It's done in the hopes of getting paid eventually, if they choose your work out of all the many applicants. But more and more, contests are only "paying" in exposure and clout. People still apply, hoping the gig will impress future employers. Musicians, high profile companies, and major sports league teams are banking on you giving them free work in return for the honor of saying that you've done work for them.

And friends, I fell for it. Years ago, I designed a t-shirt for a very popular band as part of a contest. They even chose to use my design, printing it and selling it on their very popular web store. I knew going in that it wasn't paid, but I had hoped that since it was such a high profile thing, it would surely bring me more work in the future. Their announcement would link back to my own website, I'd get increased traffic, and it would be a great portfolio piece. It was a bucket list thing to do work for this band. Maybe they'd love it and hire me for something down the road.

None of those things happened.

Well, it's a nice piece in my portfolio, but I still could have shown that design even if they'd never printed it in real life. It didn't send people flooding to my website, waving cash around and asking me to illustrate something great for them. It's never directly resulted in my getting any of the work I've gotten since. It has not made me an internet sensation. Instead, the joy of seeing a person wearing something that I created, the pride of making something for a band that people have heard of, that's supposed to be enough.

And perhaps it would be, if this weren't the thing I was trying to make my living by doing. If the rent wasn't due, and the kids didn't need to be fed, then art for its own sake would be more than enough. But that isn't the world that we live in. Now, when someone sends me a request to work for exposure, I send them a link to Mike Monteiro's "Fuck you, pay me" speech. People die of exposure.

The danger in talking about our work the way that we do, as not simply a job but our passion, is in what sociologist Andrew Ross calls "sacrificial labor"; these are jobs that are seen as meaningful or otherwise appealing, such that a worker will give up stability and benefits to pursue it.[27] This sacrifice makes leaving poor working conditions that much more difficult. Quitting a job that exploits you is even harder when it feels like you're giving up on your dreams to do so. Advocating for your own needs when you're doing important or meaningful, or even fun, work can feel selfish. *Other people have it so much worse, it doesn't feel right to complain.*

You may try to convince yourself that it's not that bad. Your work is fulfilling, after all, and that makes it all worth it. For some of these jobs, the coolness of them lies in their elite nature. They're high status and high demand, but the supply is very low and people are willing to compete for them. This makes it easier for companies to convince you to work for less, and to raise the standards to even be considered for the position. *Do you know how many people want this job? If you don't take these rates, someone else will.* Even if the working conditions or pay are terrible, they never seem to have a shortage of applicants.

Love, in the workplace, is meant to be accepted in lieu of money. But even when you love what you do, even when your work is part of who you are, it is still labor. As any parent will tell you, love can still be work. In a perfect world, we could all work solely for love.

27 Jaffe, *Work Won't Love You Back.*

With stability, free time, and resources, we could follow our bliss and nobody would be worried over a paycheck. But we don't live there, and the narrative of doing work because we love to do it is used to exploit us.

Artists, of course, are not the only ones whose work is seen as something that exists outside of capitalism. The romantic attachment of artists to their work (and I use *artist* here as a stand-in for all types of creative work) isn't so different from the love that drives care work. The way we feel about care work affects how we view the people doing that work, like teachers and nurses. Teachers have long been expected to treat their job as more than a job. It's a calling, and a calling requires dedication and extra hours, and all of that should be done out of love and care for their students. We agree that care work is absolutely essential work, but want to have it both ways and say that actually, it's not work. Raising a generation, organizing and advocating, and caring for the sick apparently aren't things that contribute to a society. Because if it isn't really work, then they don't need decent pay or benefits.

We may work as individuals, but our problems are collective ones. Some of us are in positions that make it difficult to organize for better conditions. If you're a freelancer, who is it that you're making demands to? Being a lone genius artist has a sense of romance to it, but it makes the idea of collective power hard to execute. Claire McCaughey, research manager at Canada Council for the Arts, published a paper that compares arts funding in a few different countries, and the way that it affects collective bargaining; In some countries, like Denmark, trade unions exist for artists like these. This gives them a target for their organizing efforts, a body to make demands to.[28]

We can all feel isolated in our work, whether we're artists, parents, or home health workers. We have more in common than we

28 Claire McCaughey, "Comparisons of Arts Funding in Selected Countries: Preliminary Findings," Canada Council for the Arts, October 2005, creativecity.ca/database/files/library/comparisonsofartsfunding27oct2005.pdf.

think, and when it comes to organizing, it's important to keep our shared experiences in mind. We need to take working conditions for everyone seriously. You should be able to do a job that fulfills you without having to accept a pay cut to do it, and you should understand that having a fulfilling job isn't the only way to build your life.

We've been told to do what we love, to follow our passion, and it's only one way to live. For some of us, it works out just fine. The thing that we love is also something that we can get paid to do. I love photographing people, and I would likely continue to do that whether I managed to turn it into a career or not. I truly enjoy it. The business end of things, the marketing and advertising and administrative work, I could live without. So I love part of what I do, at least, and people are willing to pay me for it.

But some of us love things that aren't marketable. It's easier to make a living if you love surgery than if you love poetry. Others don't want the headache of having to constantly search for paid work, and want their off-the-clock time to feel truly off the clock. Maybe you feel like turning your love into your income wouldn't feed your passion, but kill it. Paid work is far from the only place for people to find meaning. Maybe instead of being so set on doing what we love for our work, we should focus on building a life that we love, independent of work.

Job satisfaction isn't just about the actual tasks we're doing, but about what a job affords us. That may be giving you enough free time for hobbies you enjoy, providing your family with a comfortable life, or a balance between pay and enjoyment that is just right. If you've found yourself in a job that isn't fulfilling, but that affords you the kind of life that you want to live, you shouldn't feel like you've done things wrong. Einstein worked in a patent office. Your work can be meaningful, but it doesn't have to be. We each have to consider what we truly value, so that we can pursue those things with intention.

Inertia is a powerful thing, and it's easiest to just keep moving in the direction we're already going. Which can lead us to doing things, or aspiring toward things, that we don't truly care about because it's what we're expected to do. What we're told we should care about.

Our reasons for doing work won't all be the same, but we should fight for each other to have good working conditions all the same. Recognize that love and care can still be work, and that no one should have to accept less for sacrificial labor jobs. Love is not an acceptable substitute for compensation in the workplace. We can be deeply passionate about the work we do and still demand fair pay, and we can believe that our jobs are not our whole lives. We should find ways to fit more of what we really value into our lives, and pursue whatever work helps us to build a life that we love. In his speech to Kenyon College in 1990, Bill Watterson, creator of Calvin and Hobbes, says, "to invent your own life's meaning is not easy, but it's still allowed."[29] And it's worth the trouble.

Work Is Our Identity

It can be difficult for us to separate our work from our identity—to parse out the thing we do from who we are. We identify with the work that we do—we are artists and programmers and creatives and engineers and writers. I have spent my career as a visual artist, a creative, a designer. The labels change a bit, but at the heart of it, I make art. It's not just the work that I do, it's part of who I am. I would make art in this way whether I was paid for it or not, although I'd have much less time in my day to do it.

But people haven't always sought meaning and identity from their work. Historically, there wasn't so much emphasis on being fulfilled by our jobs. But many of us value work that's meaningful, that's impressive or interesting. Some of those sacrificial labor jobs are so desirable that people will eat any amount of shit just to put them on their resume. Saying that you work for a tech colossus like Google or Apple is worth it, no matter what the actual work conditions are

29 Bill Watterson, "Some Thoughts on the Real World by One Who Glimpsed It and Fled," Kenyon College Commencement address, May 20, 1990, web.mit.edu/jmorzins/www/C-H-speech.html.

like. Doing the kind of work that these companies produce, working on projects that are not only interesting but might be changing the landscape in a positive way—that's meaningful. When you feel like your work is who you are, you want that work to matter. But we are more than just our social uses.

Just as we need to consider what we really value in life, we also need to consider what our work actually means to us. To think about which aspects of ourselves are connected to our work, and to realize that those parts of us exist whether we're being paid for them or not. Our jobs might allow us to use our creativity and imagination, or to help people. But there are other ways to meet those needs in our lives, and to connect those things to our identities independent of a job. All the parts of ourselves that we bring to our work still exist without it; they still make us a whole person.

While some of us identify really strongly with the work that we do, we can also experience work as an obstacle to living our lives, rather than as an integrated part of our lives. Rachel Hands manages teams of people building tech tools to support non-profit organizations, and also writes about work on her own website. In a piece called *On Dreaming of Labor*, she writes that we all have different reasons for working: we work because we need money, or because it's fun—because we're curious, or because we care about the things that need tended to and about the people around us, or because we have something to share, or just because we're really good at the thing that we do.[30]

We don't all want the same things out of our work. But all of the things that we want, except the paycheck, can be true whether they're tied to a job or not. We are still curious, we still care, we are still good at what we do even if we don't do those things in the service of a job. When people lose a job, through layoffs or disability, they so often feel

30 Rachel Hands, "On Dreaming of Labor," RachelHands.com, January 25, 2024, rachelhands.com/2024/01/25/on-dreaming-of-labor/.

like they've lost a core part of who they are. In those moments, we must remember we are still the same person, with or without our jobs.

We are more than just our social uses. More than our contribution to the common utility. We are deserving of shelter, food, and rest regardless of our "use" to society. Disabled people, parents, children, the elderly, people who have been displaced from their jobs by automation—we all deserve those things whether we're employed or not. We do not have to earn our worth.

Instead, we can strive to make work better, and to make our cultural ideas about work more realistic, to separate what we do from who we are. We can assess what we need to do the best job, but also identify the things that we need to thrive in all areas of our lives. We need to stop defining success in terms of how our work is going, but by how the whole of our lives are going.

What do we have to give up to get the things that we really need? We may need to let go of the idea that a job should be our whole identity, to seek fulfillment elsewhere in our lives. We may need to give up identifying so strongly with the work that we do, that we'll accept being underpaid and overworked, that we keep doing work that is slowly killing us. We may need to give up celebrating jobs that exploit us.

Personal Brands

When our sense of identity is so tied to the work that we do, we become our own personal brands. We create a product, but we also are the product, we are the content, we are the brand. And therefore, we are burned out because the work never really stops. Every hour of the day is an opportunity for content generation, so you're never truly off the clock. I have so many instagrams, niched down to different audiences, for different services, and it's a job all on its own. Leisure time is work, now, because your whole life is work now. Social media isn't a fun space to goof around—it's a place we leverage to market ourselves, to build our platform, whether we want to or not.

Self-promotion isn't something that comes naturally to everyone; it's why "I made a thing" became a social media trope. We feel kind of gross, plying our wares to the void of the internet like a door to door salesman. But if we don't do it, no one else will.

So we hedge. *It's not a big deal, you can read it if you want, it's whatever.* We might feel that all this self-promoting is morally complicated, but from a strictly process point of view, technology has made building your brand around the clock super easy. There was once a time when if I wanted to show a painting to someone else who lived far away, I'd have to buy film, take a photo, finish off the roll, send it out to be developed, have prints made, and then mail it to them. There could be weeks between when I finished that painting and when someone else saw it. This makes me sound old, and I am. But even in the early days of the internet, I'd have to get out the digital camera, transfer the files to my desktop computer, and then upload them to LiveJournal.

These days, I can do every step of the process from my phone. I take the picture with it, maybe I'll edit it, and then I can share it with everyone around the globe instantly. I can manage my many instagrams from my couch. There's little that I can't do directly from my phone, and since I can, I do. When your love is your work, and you are your brand, there's no delineation, and it makes setting boundaries difficult.

It's also hard not to let your own self-worth get tangled up in the success of the product (because you are the product), and so much of that is out of your hands. Shifting trends in the market and other unforeseen obstacles mean that your livelihood can just collapse. I worked primarily as a wedding photographer when Covid hit. I didn't get hired less because my work had gotten worse, or my marketing was ineffective, there was a global pandemic where I suddenly couldn't be within six feet of people. I can't photograph a wedding unless there is a wedding to photograph. You may find that your primary source of income is affected by changes in algorithms on social media sites that you once relied upon for work, or companies who used to hire actual illustrators switching to AI-generated images. When you are the product, and the product fails, it's hard not to feel like you have failed.

Brad Stulberg, author of the *Passion Paradox*, worries in his article on burnout for Outside Online that our identity, our sense of self, becomes something very fragile when we focus so much on external forces that we don't have any control over.[31]

This kind of environment also makes it easy to find ourselves in a place where we're forced to focus on external validation. We may have started out writing because we loved the process of it, but eventually we need all the little pings of attention we get when we share what we've written online. Maybe that sounds shallow to you, and you can't imagine a world where you'd care about how many likes something gets.

But when you're a brand, not a person, that recognition is necessary to be able to keep doing your job. Many kinds of artists used to have someone else who worried about these things—a publisher, a magazine, a record company. It was a public relations problem that had nothing to do with them. They made the work, and it was someone else's job to make sure that people saw that work and paid for it. Other kinds of artists were paid by grants or residencies, and didn't have to worry over the marketability of what they created. Hemingway never had to consider what the best time to post links to his new article would be, or follow the changing demands of every platform's different algorithms.

But we do. Now that artists can connect directly with their fans over social media, the people who can both create something and market it effectively are the ones who are succeeding. Those who can't, or don't want to, are struggling. Some of us balk at the idea of

31 Brad Stulberg, "A Simple Solution to Millennial Burnout," OutsideOnline.com, May 3, 2019, outsideonline.com/health/training-performance/millennial-burn-out-causes-solution/.

marketing our own work because it truly is an entirely separate job, and doing it means we have less time to do our actual work.

I already have to plan a session, photograph it, edit it, and deliver it to the people who paid me for it. Now I've got to research trending sounds on TikTok and produce videos that are interesting and relatable, and set up a near constant stream of content to find new clients.

Now, the upside to social media is the lack of gatekeeping, the democratization of attention. You don't have to be published in a magazine, you can publish your own self right there on the internet! Anyone can go viral!

We've been sold on the autonomy and independence that we get from social media. You're your own boss, and you're in charge. But that also means that you have no one else looking out for you, *you're in charge*. You're expected to take on all the risk. People are learning in real time that the platform they've spent years building their audience on could simply disappear tomorrow.

Even if you do have a boss, you aren't exempt. Your entire office is still on your phone, ready to go wherever you do. You might not be expected to be popular on TikTok, but you work to produce evidence that you're working, by being available on Slack and sending emails at all hours of the day. The brand you're building is of an engaged and involved worker, and the boundaries between your work and your life blur.

Maybe the call is coming from inside of the house, and we are inflicting all this work on ourselves. We've given our jobs an outsized hold over our lives, expecting to find meaning and identity in our work. When we sell ourselves as a brand, we become literally inseparable from our work. We are what we do, and that means we have to do whatever it takes, including any amount of overwork, to keep our jobs. Who are we without them?

Morality of Work

It's not just that our identity is tied to our work, our moral framework is too. Here in America, we have a certain ideology about work. It's one of the few things our society at large appears to agree on, and there are only a few simple, common sense rules. Number one, work is good. Therefore anyone who doesn't work, with the exception of babies, perhaps, is not good. Two, more work is better. Three, we are self-reliant and we do not require help from anyone.

Working is a thing to be proud of, and overworking even more so. We even reward hard work in our cartoons, where Thomas the Tank Engine teaches us that the only good train is a useful one. Is it any wonder then, when people curate their social media existence, it's focused on hashtag hustlin'?

Protestants made an entire religion of it, believing that hard work was a calling, and that your reward would await you in heaven. You weren't meant to work so that you could be happy, or fulfilled, or even to pay your bills, really. You worked to be good. Work is our country's ultimate virtue, and at the end of the day, it doesn't really matter what we're working on or why. It only matters that we are.

These concepts and ideals that we attribute to common sense, or human nature, came from somewhere. So who decided that a productive person is a virtuous one?

Our values about work and leisure are different now than they were fifty or one hundred or five hundred years ago. This statement sounds incredibly obvious on an intellectual level, but it can be easy to fall into the trap of thinking that what we do now is what we've always done, and that obviously it's what people believe. It's human nature.

But how we should live our lives has always been a topic of debate. Where we view leisure as lazy idle time now, ancient Greeks saw an inability to rest as its own kind of idleness. They would look at us, frantically buzzing around answering phone calls while we eat our lunch, as self-destructive. The need for busywork, the need to look productive, was something they called *acedia.* Acedia was a sadness, deep in the soul. A state where a person was not at one with themselves.

The Greeks didn't have a word for work, exactly. There was leisure, and there was not-leisure. Not-leisure was the everyday work of the world. Greek life was built around leisure, an idea that Aristotle wrote about in his *Politics.* For them, work didn't have any moral attachment, it was simply a thing people had to do sometimes so that they could get back to their actual lives.

Antisthenes, a contemporary of Plato, on the other hand, equated effort with goodness and virtue. Like the Protestants after him, he thought that we worked because it made us good, that it was morally right to be working. In his essay on leisure, Josef Pieper calls Antisthenes the world's first workaholic.[32]

Immanuel Kant, however, would argue that neither of these guys were doing any work. In Aristotle's time, thinking was seen as a paradise. You couldn't get any farther away from working than you could when you were thinking. Romantic philosophers relied on intuition and insight—they believed ideas simply arrived in their brains. In *Leisure: the Basis of Culture,* Pieper's interpretation of Kant's arguments was that romantic philosophy was not work, and that thinking was working: it was an active process, and one that took great effort. The effort was the thing that made knowing something valuable; it was what made philosophy legitimate.[33]

Kant's concept of what we'd now call "knowledge work" is one that is exclusively an active process. Intellectual labor rests on this idea that any knowing must come from doing, and that the effort we put into knowing something determines its truth and its value. It is at odds with the romantic philosopher, as it is with the creative artist.

---

32 Joseph Pieper, *Leisure: The Basis of Culture, 1st edition* (Ignatius Press, 2009).
33 Ibid

If an artist is struck by creative inspiration, is that work less than one made through active intellectual work? Is that any way to judge art?

The idea that simply receiving knowledge or ideas—the insight of the romantic philosopher, the inspiration of artists—didn't cost anything is suspect. Vision is, by its very nature, effortless. Kant felt that without effort, there couldn't be any real gain in it. Today, we simply cannot accept that a person should receive something that they have not suffered for.

This philosophy is why people see it as common sense that anything good has to be difficult. In fact, the harder something is to do, the greater the moral good. Anything that a person does just because they feel like it must not be moral or worthwhile, because it didn't cost them anything. The flip side of that is that humans just don't trust something that comes without effort. You can't accept anything that you haven't gained yourself, through painful effort, and must refuse anything undeserved. In short, we stole our sense of rugged American individualism from a German guy.

There is a common idea in Christianity that the highest form of love is to love one's enemy. Kant would say that's the case because you're repressing your natural feelings toward your enemy, and that struggle is what makes it such a moral good. Something can't be that hard without also being moral.

But Thomas Aquinas would say that virtue doesn't lie in how hard something is to do. That, in fact, we *do* good simply because we *are* good. Our inherent goodness means that anything we'd be naturally inclined to do must also be moral. That our virtue has perfected us, and so doing something of the highest moral good would come to us without effort.

So do we work because we're moral, or are we moral because we work?

Perhaps the answer is neither. People's dignity and worth are entirely separate from their employment status. Pope John Paul II, arguably an authority on morality, wrote in *Laborem Exercens* that work only has dignity because people do. Work does not dignify us, we dignify work.

Perhaps the Greeks were onto something, viewing work itself as morally neutral. Simply a thing that we do when it needs to be done, and not something to be valorized, nor something that determines our goodness.

Human beings have inherent dignity; we matter because we exist, not because we labor. Our work isn't only worth something if we suffer for it, and our working conditions should measure up to our dignity, as we embrace alternative ideas of work's role in a life well-lived. Considering these alternative ideas, and making real change in the way that we work, means taking a good look at our beliefs around the morality of work.

The Fear

We may inflict some of this devotion to overwork on ourselves, but that doesn't mean we don't have some very compelling reasons to do so.

In part, we may feel the need to prove our productivity because of our sense of morality, that we are good people and thus we must work hard all of the time. A culture that tells us we're doing the right thing by working constantly is definitely a factor.

But our devotion to overwork also comes from what a friend calls "The Fear." We're afraid that if we lose this job, there won't be another one, or maybe the next one will be worse. We're afraid that we could be let go at any time, reading articles every day about another company that got bought out and has laid off most of its staff. We're also reading articles about how no one wants to work anymore, that those workers who've grown tired of being exploited and want out of the grind are lazy and spoiled.

Our culture values a devotion to work, telling us that hard work will be rewarded with success. But it doesn't value the actual people doing the work, at least not enough to pay them a fair wage or give them a safe workplace. We are burned out because the gap between our ideals and our realities just keeps growing.

Because our work feels so precarious, we feel like we can't turn down any opportunity to make money, because it may not always be there. There's a pressure to get paid for your time, all of it. Even if it hasn't been financially necessary for me to take offered work, I felt like I had to. I could get laid off, or struggle to find a freelance gig when this one is up, so we have to make hay while the sun shines.

Thanks to technology, the sun is always shining.

There was a time when you had to physically go to a factory or an office to do more work; the hours that you could be laboring for money were limited. But knowledge work truly allows you to work from anywhere you are, every hour of the day. Hours that you aren't working can feel like a lost opportunity. But it's not sustainable to work every moment of your day, even if it is technically possible.

We are steeped in a culture that not only tells us that it's good and moral to work long hours, but that it may be the only thing saving us from the next round of layoffs. So we just never stop. We take our work phones on vacation with us, and respond to requests that absolutely aren't emergencies. Many of us live on call, able to be pinged at any time, even on our days off.

A boss of mine once said, "There's no such thing as a design emergency," which he is extremely correct about. Yet we treat everyone as an essential worker now. We are as unlikely as ever to take the vacation time that's supposedly available to us, according to surveys cited in Meghan McCarty Carino's article in *Marketplace*, and when we do manage to get away, most of us work through it.[34]

34 Meghan McCarty Carino, "Workers Are Putting off Vacation as Pandemic Increases Stress," *Marketplace*, August 17, 2020, marketplace.org/2020/08/17/workers-putting-off-vacation-pandemic-increases-stress

Why can't we leave the office at the office (or the work share, or the desk in our kitchen, or wherever we do our work these days)? We're worried that we'll get behind on our work. We may be the only person even performing a particular function at our workplace—I've worked at more than one place where I was the only designer. That means that you have to do double the work so that things can carry on in your absence, only to return to a stack of work that built up while you were gone. It may not feel worth it to take the time off, only to have to bookend it with burnout.

More worryingly, some people have reported that they don't take vacations out of devotion to the company. It's an opportunity to show what work machines they are. They simply don't need breaks. Ego may lead them to feel indispensable, or job insecurity may make them want to appear indispensable. They may worry that their workplace would carry on just fine without them. Whatever their reasons, they feel like they aren't able to take any real meaningful breaks from work.

It's the primary narrative for success. Startup founders and billionaires will tell you that they got to where they are by giving up sleep, family time, and whatever else they had to so that they could fill more hours with work. We're told, again and again, that our success also lies in our ability to hustle, to work more hours than the next person.

But the reason that CEOs praise overwork is that they are the ones who profit from your time. They own the company, and they see the profits from any work they put in, as well as all the work that you put in. It may be true that they built their empire by working all of the time, but they also got to reap the reward of that empire. Now, they want to convince us that hustle is good, so that they can profit from our labor as much as possible before we burn out.

We're not just working all the time because Jeff Bezos says we should, of course. The Fear is fed by a history of layoffs and downsizing. In *The Overworked American*, economist Juliet B. Schor writes that the hours we spend working have steadily increased since the 1970s, which is when consultants began preaching that the best way to cut costs was to fire as many employees as you could.[35] Everyone felt they had to prove their worth to their bosses. Then, when the consultants were making their recommendations for cuts, your name wouldn't come up. The easiest way to show that you were a hard worker, someone worth keeping, was to stay later than the guy next to you. Companies hired less people and simply expected them to do more. I once held a job that had folded in the responsibilities of an entire eight-person department. This is not a brag; it's terrible management.

This pressure to perform at a high level, feeling like our jobs are always on the line, is crushing us. But it feels inescapable. We work more than is healthy because we don't feel that our jobs are secure, or because it's the path to success that we've been sold. Because we're told it's the moral thing to do, or because we're afraid the work won't be there later on. Hustle culture tells us that being overworked and constantly accessible is just the price of success, and The Fear drives us to keep offering up more of our lives to work.

Invisible Effort

Proving our productivity, our worth as a worker, can be harder for those of us doing knowledge work. It's a strange categorization, because what work doesn't require using knowledge? But the term is meant to encompass work that's largely not observable, with its progress difficult to quantify. And many of us are doing knowledge work for a living.

I'm doing it right now, in fact. For an outside observer, it's hard to see how me sitting in a park and staring into space could possibly qualify as work. There's a joke in *Mad Men*, where the boss comes in and Don Draper, ad man extraordinaire, is stretched out on a couch. The boss says, "I can never get used to the fact that most of the time it looks like you're doing nothing."

35 Juliet B. Schor, *The Overworked American: The Unexpected Decline in Leisure* (Basic Books, 1993).

But that is the essence of knowledge work, you can't really see the thing that's being done. You can't see a person thinking. You can see them sitting, or holding a book, or in the case of *Mad Men*, drinking scotch. But you can't see their thought process. You can't quantify their work, or measure their progress. To an outside observer, there's no effort happening here, so how can we then attach a value to your labor? How can you prove that you're even working?

Kant's suggestion that effort is what makes knowledge work valid and valuable is at the heart of our tendency not to view creative work as real work. My workday doesn't appear to involve that much effort, really. I press buttons on a camera. I sit at a desk, and click different buttons on a mouse. In the photography world, customers often balk at the price of an 8x10, because when they print their own photos, it runs them about $5.

But they're not paying us for the paper, they are paying us for what's printed on it, and that is more difficult to attach a value to. The work isn't in the button pressing, but in the active reasoning that happens before the button pressing. Composition, understanding the way that light works, setting aperture and shutter speed to accomplish a vision—none of this work is visible. All this active work goes hand in hand with the inspiration for posing a subject or choosing an interesting angle that results in the final product. Vision and effort and invisible knowledge work are all part of the job that I'm doing. Naturally, I'm in favor of a worldview that doesn't dismiss big components of what I'm doing as "not work."

Nearly every job involves some level of invisible effort, and modern work often values the proof of work more than even the work itself. This results in us having to perform a lot of busywork, just to prove that we're doing something. Value is gauged not by the work you've produced, but by how much you look like you're been doing, by the perception of effort. Which means that so much of the work we do every day only serves to show someone else that we're sufficiently busy, and it leaves us with less time to do actual useful work. The work we're supposed to be doing is being undermined by this need to prove it.

Behavioral economist Dan Ariely told a story on his blog about a locksmith, who was getting more complaints about his prices as he got better at his job. He was so quick to unlock a door now, that his customers "felt cheated."[36] You'd expect a customer to be happy that he could work so fast—how long do you really want to stand around, locked out of your home or car? But they felt that since it was so easy for him, it was unfair that they should have to pay so much. Good work, meaningful work, doesn't have to mean a great visible effort. Whether it takes you five hours or five minutes, if you've unlocked the door, then you did the job. Oliver Burkeman, author of *Four Thousand Weeks*, calls this the "Effort Trap" in a piece titled *Nobody Cares How Hard You Work.*[37] When work is done quickly, others are less likely to value it—no matter how great the outcome—because they aren't seeing the effort. It's like the famous story of a woman objecting to the price of a Picasso sketch, complaining that it only took him thirty seconds. *No*, Picasso says, *it took me my whole life.* Our gut tells us that a thing done quickly isn't worth much, even if it was done very, very well. We can't just do a good job, even a great job. We must also show that we've put in enough effort. We must show that we've suffered, that the work came at a cost to us.

It's difficult to quantify knowledge work, but it's easy to quantify time spent, and monitoring your time is something that companies are doing more across every industry. Doctors and Starbucks baristas can now share in having a computer surveilling every minute of their day. Nursing home workers and Amazon drivers alike complain about a lack of control at work, where they don't even have enough time to use the bathroom. Most places are turning to tech solutions that help

36 Dan Ariely, "Locksmiths," DanAriely.com, December 15, 2010, danariely.com/locksmiths/.

37 Oliver Burkeman, "Nobody Cares How Hard You Work," Behance.net, October 14, 2015, behance.net/blog/nobody-cares-how-hard-you-work.

them to micromanage their employees, to ensure they aren't paying for a second of your time that you aren't working.

UnitedHealth uses a system that logs their employees' computer keystrokes and mouse movements, as a way to prove their productivity. Their social workers were often penalized for being idle while they counseled their patients, because doing that work doesn't involve much interaction with the computer. But their job, their core responsibility, is to counsel patients. To talk to them. Some social workers resorted to mindlessly tapping keys just to make the system acknowledge that they were working, so that they could get paid. This need to prove productivity makes it difficult to do core parts of the job. Instead of actually helping a patient, these professionals were distracted by the need to scoot a mouse around and type something, anything, to prove that they were working when they were working.

"We're in this era of measurement, but we don't know what we should be measuring," said Ryan Fuller, former vice president for workplace intelligence at Microsoft, in a *New York Times* article on worker productivity tracking. Some jobs would seem to defy this kind of measuring, like that of a hospice chaplain. How can you possibly measure the good that someone does offering spiritual care for the dying? Through productivity points, it turns out. According to that same article, visiting a dying person would earn you a point, but a phone call to a grieving family was only a quarter point. Participating in a funeral would earn you nearly two points. One chaplain admitted to doing what they called a "spiritual drive by." If a patient was asleep, they could ask the nurse if there were any concerns, and earn half a point for the visit.[38] But death defies planning. Some patients needed more time, some canceled appointments, others died when they were not scheduled to do so. Chaplains are forced to decide between earning enough points for the day and seeing the patients who really needed them. When your job is to help patients wrestle with deep,

38 Jodie Kantor and Arya Sundaram, "The Rise of the Worker Productivity Score," *New York Times*, August 14, 2022, nytimes.com/interactive/2022/08/14/business/worker-productivity-tracking.html.

meaningful questions like "How do I face my own death?", the idea of reducing that work to a point system is ghoulish. To have to leave a patient coming to terms with their cancer diagnosis, and the idea of potentially leaving behind their young children, because you have to fit in four more points to meet your quota sounds like a bad joke. Reducing our lives to some stats on a spreadsheet makes us less human.

While I was reading the *New York Times* article that gave me that information about hospital chaplains, the website showed me a little pop-up to inform me that I was being tracked. The *New York Times* was giving me a productivity score, with warnings while I scrolled that I'd become idle, and that it might count against me. Even though I wasn't being paid to read the article, and they can't actually do anything to me, it was stressful. My status dropped to idle pretty frequently while reading the article, which is the thing that I was supposed to be doing. I could improve my score by mindlessly moving my mouse around, even though that does nothing at all to improve my reading comprehension. It isn't making me do my "job" any better or resulting in my spending any more time "working." It's an entirely unnecessary distraction to actually reading the article. My grade was deemed "acceptable," with less than 40% of my time spent idling, and a reading time that suggested comprehension. I had proved, to the tracking software's satisfaction, that I was being productive

Being micromanaged is demoralizing, and thanks to software like this, you don't even have to go to the office to have someone micromanage you. Companies want you to account for every second that you're there, and to make sure that you aren't wasting any of their time.

When Carol Kramer, a finance executive, took a new job that used tracking software, they would only pay her for time that the system thought she was working. But again, these systems can only really track things like key presses and mouse movement, things done on the computer. Anything else—reading, thinking, even doing math on paper—did not count, even though many of these things are core parts of doing her job. Since none of that work counted as work, she had to put in more hours. "You have to be in front of your computer, in work mode, for 55 or 60 hours just to get those 40 hours counted and paid for," she said in the *New York Times*. Workers are not being paid for the time that they are absolutely working. Is it any wonder that Carol said "there was never any trust that you were working for the team."[39]

These systems are often used to penalize workers. I worked for a call center that logged every second of my entire day there. I was allowed a minute and a half after a call ended, to type up notes from the call, before I had to hop on another one. I was allowed three five-minute bathroom breaks a day. We were timed during our calls, to make sure that our actual work wasn't taking too long either. For desktop support, our average call time had to be under seven minutes.

All of this tracking and surveillance made me worse at my job. Aside from building resentment for being constantly monitored, I routinely got feedback from customers who felt that they were rushed. They *were* rushed; it was my job to rush them. I was reprimanded if my calls ran too long, and I was reprimanded for one-star reviews from unhappy customers, and I didn't feel like there was any way that I could succeed there.

To keep our call time averages down, we would often have people restart their computers and then call us back when it was finished, rather than stay on the line and have dead air. They'd have to call back, get a different agent in a different call center, and explain their problem all over again. Employees are miserable, and customers are getting terrible service, but at least the company can be sure that I haven't wasted twenty extra seconds getting a drink of water.

Working under constant surveillance is demonstrably bad for us. Perhaps you think that I'm being overly dramatic, it's just a little timer

39 Kantor and Sundaram, "Worker Productivity," nytimes.com/interactive/2022/08/14/business/worker-productivity-tracking.html

after all. *So what if you don't even have control over your own bathroom usage?*

I'd like to introduce you to something that Henry Harlow created, called the pit of despair. A comparative psychologist, Harlow wanted to trigger depression in animals, for science. The pit had everything that a monkey could need to technically survive—food and water—and nothing else. For the first day or two, the monkeys would try to climb out, but they would just keep sliding down the sides of the pit. Within a few days, they had given up, and spent their time huddled in the corner. They had lost hope, and become depressed. Another scientist wrote that he hadn't seen a single monkey that had any defense against the pit of despair, they all came out damaged.

What does this have to do with your work surveilling you? Hopelessness breeds despair, and taking all control away from a person (or a monkey) breeds hopelessness. Workers are constantly supervised, and red lights and alarms will let them know that they aren't keeping up. Their schedules are determined by algorithms that intentionally don't schedule enough staff for the work that needs to be done. They're penalized by digital time clocks for being ten seconds late. Break rooms are plastered with signs telling employees not to clock in until after they've removed their coats and stashed their things in lockers—take your coat off on your own time. Schedules are unstable and change on little notice. They don't have control over their work lives, it makes them feel powerless, and they slide back into the pit of despair. It's inhumane, but it's profitable, and these tactics are finding their ways into more and more types of work. No wonder gig work seems so alluring.

We are not monkeys, of course. But the feeling that we don't have real autonomy in our work leaves us burned out. The need to prove that we're being productive every second of our workday—whether to a manager or a machine—makes us feel like our bosses don't trust us, and maybe don't even understand what goes into the work that we do. Our work requires us to think, to plan, to consider, to assess, and none of these are things that we can truly prove that we're doing. What we have to show for our work is the eventual outcome. The effort—the part that can't be quantified, tracked, and subsequently valued—is invisible.

Shifting Risks

We used to expect a company to absorb more risk than they do today. They were the ones reaping most of the reward, after all. As a society, we developed a safety net for things like unemployment or disability. Those risks were shared, because we thought that these burdens were too much for a person to bear individually, and this was enforced by unions and government regulations. At that time, the dominant business model was one where company stock was rooted in long-term projections—they were stable, steady things. Employers set aside funds in a pool of money to invest, and when employees retired, they would get a pension. It was a guaranteed amount, regardless of how the investments had performed, so if a stock tanked, the employer ate that cost. The employee would still get their full pension, so the company absorbed the risk.

In her book *Can't Even*, Anne Helen Petersen explains how moving away from that model is largely responsible for companies shifting economic risks back to their workers, and how companies came to be so focused on short-term gains. Companies stopped offering pension plans to their employees, asking them to invest in mutual funds through their 401k instead. If one of those stocks would tank, it's the employee who now has less money in their retirement fund. The worker is absorbing the risk. As Petersen writes, what seems like a minor change shaped the entire market's mindset, rewarding short-term profits over long-term stability, because those short-term profits showed up as gains in their 401k statements.[40]

Where once a company making a small but steady profit was the goal, that is now seen as failure. They're expected to increase

40 Anne Helen Petersen, *Can't Even: How Millennials Became the Burnout Generation* (Dey Street Books, 2020).

profits, every year, forever. This is essentially impossible, and it leads to companies making bad long-term decisions for those short-term wins. They've gotten as lean as possible, and then leaner still, aiming for the smallest and cheapest staff to cut their costs.

Employees are essential to a business—the company needs them to generate profits. But employees are also an expense, and a large one for most businesses. Every employee they cut meant a little less money spent for their wages and benefits, even if it meant that it would be harder for them to generate profits down the road. *That's later, and we're trying to save money now.* The short-term profits they saw from employee cuts would make their stock prices go up, and their shareholders would be happy.

Cutting employees may help the stock market to thrive, but it makes our working conditions worse. It's significantly harder to do the job of four people day after day. But no one is scaling back on the work when these employees are let go, so it just gets absorbed by the staff that's still there. *Sorry that you have to run an entire Wendy's during the lunch rush by yourself, but the company saves a lot of money by understaffing.* Consultants who will absolutely never have to do this kind of work look at things from a purely capitalistic point of view. Workers are a big expense, and when you're trying to increase your profit margins as much as possible, the math says to have fewer workers. There's no room in this model to consider what actually working there is going to be like as a result. If the goal is infinite growth at all costs, then employees are just exploitable entities as long as the line goes up.

Restaurants and retail stores used to just schedule a set amount of employees, who could expect their schedule to be fairly static as well as their paychecks. Perhaps they'd send a few people home if things were slow. But generally, you could plan for things like childcare, and budget for your bills. These companies absorbed the risk of paying some employees for time that they didn't really need them. Now, these places are increasingly using algorithmic scheduling software to pay the least amount of employees they can get away with for a shift. Their workers take on the risk, often having to scramble to arrange childcare from week to week as their schedule constantly changes. If things are slow at the restaurant, that's now the workers' problem.

Barbara Ehrenreich, author and political activist, argues that the working poor are actually the major philanthropists of our society. When someone is working for less than they can live on, they've made a great sacrifice to you, so that you can live more cheaply and conveniently: "To be a member of the working poor is to be an anonymous donor, a nameless benefactor, to everyone else."[41] Just because people are desperate enough to accept exploitative conditions doesn't make the conditions any less exploitative.

Workers take on the risk of a changing stock market, the looming specter of layoffs, and pay that's dependent on how the business is performing. They're also taking on the expense of their training, and the risk that it won't pay off for them. Historically, it's been common to train on the job, working your way up in the company by doing so. In some industries, this is still very common. In many others, you're expected to pay for college, maybe graduate school, and certificate programs, and to work unpaid internships without any assurance that you'll get a return on that investment. When I finished graduate school with degrees in design and film, I sent out a mountain of resumes. So did everyone else. This was during the recession in 2008, and a colleague at a place I'd once interned said that they'd had to close a job listing after just two days, because they'd received hundreds of resumes for that one position. I heard a similar story more recently, in 2025, where a company received 650 resumes for a position in just 48 hours.

You could argue that I had brought this on myself, by getting not one but two art degrees, but that is an argument for a different book. What's at least somewhat relevant here is that I had graduated

41 Barbara Ehrenreich, *Nickel and Dimed: On (Not) Getting By in America* (Picador, 2011).

magna cum laude from our university honors program. I had great references, I had earned multiple scholarships. I did all of the things that I was told would lead to a fulfilling and financially stable career. I ended up finding work at a factory that makes sports jerseys, then a call center, then a veterinary clinic. I worked a second unpaid internship in the hopes that it would someday turn into work, and I did get two contract gigs for a few months each from the contacts I'd made there. The first job in my field that I was actually paid to do was a part-time contract gig, doing layouts for explanation of benefits documents, which I fit in around my schedule at the vet. I eventually landed my first full-time job in my field that offered benefits three years after I finished my MFA, and I know that some of you will read this and think, *Only three years? That's not bad.* We are told many things will lead to success and prosperity—working hard, getting a degree, meritocracy—but our life experiences are showing us otherwise.

Work is often part of our education, as many programs require internships. We're told we can't be exploited, because we aren't really workers at all. When graduate students, who teach classes and grade assignments while doing their own research, tried to unionize, they were told that their work wasn't really work. They're not paid a wage; they're given grants toward their education. So their labor is a privilege, and not work.

This is something sociologist Erin Hatton calls "status coercion," and it's often applied to other workers like prison laborers and student athletes. If you don't get a paycheck, you're not a worker. And since you're not a worker, your status as some other thing allows your superiors to have more punitive power than most bosses have. Generally, the worst your boss can do to you is to fire you. But the future employment of those grad students, even the actual conferral of their degree, depends on the advisors for whom they work. Those advisors can delay their graduation or dismiss them from the program altogether.

Medical interns are also supposedly not really working, which I'm sure is news to them. Since interning is a part of their education, it's not really work, and so some argue that it shouldn't be subject to complaints about labor practices. Students then need to find work outside of these not-quite-jobs, but as these not-quite-jobs take up significant hours, and they're still required to actually study as well, how can they fit it all in?

Hustle culture tells us that more work is better, but there are a finite number of hours in a day. Unpaid internships, graduate work, even medical school become things that can only be done by people who come from money. Most of us simply can't afford to work for free.

While companies shift more and more risk onto their employees, and even try to argue that their employees are not real employees, they aren't passing along the rewards. Chasing short-term profits means that they no longer see their workers as assets, people that they should have some loyalty to, but as a line item in their budget. When the company does well, those profits go toward increasing an already huge CEO salary, so the ratio between their paycheck and yours gets ever higher.

The Gig Economy and Voluntary Workers

Some of us feel lucky to only have one job that's exploiting us. Thanks to the gig economy, many of us have built careers that are really just three jobs in a trenchcoat. We continue to expect more out of our work, that it will give us meaning and purpose. Instead, we're scrambling to fill all the hours that we can work with side hustles and gigs.

Somehow, our society remains convinced that many of us taking part in the gig economy are doing it for funsies. Like temp workers before us (and many fast food workers today), gig workers are often viewed as voluntary workers. *These aren't people who need a job to pay bills or feed their families, they're high school kids, retirees. People who just like to have a little extra cash.*

We don't view these jobs as real work, but more of a hobby. At least that's how the commercials advertising them make them look. Here's a woman having a nice conversation while she drives around the city for a rideshare company. There's a friendly retired couple who are happy to share their garage apartment with travelers on vacation. It's sold as a nice way for people to use their skills or their resources, to sell a service at a price that they set. What temp workers and gig workers have in common is that companies don't really feel like they owe these people anything, because they aren't really employees.

Contract and freelance work isn't all downsides, of course. These jobs started out offering autonomy and independence. You made your own hours, forged your own path. A hired gun, loyal to no man. It fits well into our culture of rugged individualism and self-reliance. Certainly, some of us have worked freelance opportunities that have felt this way. We were able to charge a fair rate, and worked hours that we set. But increasingly, companies want to have it both ways. They want freelance workers to accept the downsides, like a lack of job stability and the risk of not having a set amount of hours, but they also don't want them to have the benefits they once did. Technically, it isn't legal for a company to control the schedule of their contract workers, yet many of them try to anyway. They don't want to pay you like a regular employee, but they do want to control you like one.

In a regular office job, even a non-salaried one, you get paid for the full day, even if you're spending time reading the news or drinking your coffee. But when you're doing gig work, that isn't billable time. If you're driving for Lyft, you're only getting paid for the minutes that you spend driving. Any other aspects of your job—getting gas, driving to your pickup location, waiting for fares, eating lunch—is not time that you are paid for. Time off, for any reason, is lost wages.

Working for yourself seems like it should mean that you can take a vacation whenever you want to, but mostly it means that you never do. This security is what you're typically giving up in exchange for that autonomy, but increasingly companies want to give you neither. Though they've shifted all the risk to these contract and gig workers, companies still expect them to behave like regular employees, ideal workers, even. They want it both ways.

Uber famously tried to argue that they are a tech company, and that their drivers are not their employees. You see, drivers are consumers of the app, just like passengers are. They aren't employees, and Uber has no need to treat them as though they are. As Alex Rosenblat explains in his book *Uberland*, that means that they don't have to pay a minimum wage, offer benefits, pay employment taxes, or offer any job security at all. Uber gets all of the cash and takes on none of the risk.[42] Legally, they owe you nothing. If they can frame their business as though it isn't a primary source of income for some people, then it's easy for them to ignore that their workers can't make ends meet.

We do the same thing when we frame fast food jobs as something that high schoolers do to have a little disposable income, and not a regular job that people need to feed their families. If it's just a little fun money, and not someone's livelihood, it's easier to ignore that the company is taking advantage of them. What used to be an outlier in the work sphere—freelancing and gig work—is becoming the model for everyone. Full-time jobs continue to drift toward more precarious gigs and contract work. Employers expect you to act like a manager, to be involved and take ownership of your work and the company's well-being. But they don't want to pay you like a manager, or give you the benefits that a manager would have. All the responsibility with none of the reward. It's not uncommon for companies to ask this of workers, while dangling promotions if you keep up the good work. Likewise, they want to take on none of the risk of hiring a full-time employee (the added expense of full-time benefits, guaranteeing some

---

42 Alex Rosenblat, *Uberland: How Algorithms Are Rewiring the Rules of Work* (Oakland: University of California Press, 2018), 203.

security) but still reap all the rewards of having one (control over your schedule, work on demand only when they need it).

It's a big change from the days when companies used to actually employ all of the people who worked there, which meant that those people were also receiving benefits.It's great for employees, but more expensive for the company, so they eventually started hiring temps. Many of the people who keep a place running—cleaners, lunch staff, payroll, lawn maintenance, even customer service—don't actually work for that company anymore. They're hired by a temp agency. They're gig workers.

I used to work as a tech support agent for Apple products. But I didn't actually work for Apple at all, I worked for Teletech, which led to a lot of confusion from customers. They thought that they were speaking to someone at the Genius Bar, but instead, they were talking to a high school kid with a few weeks of training and access to Google. It's confusing for the workers as well. If you're an IT technician working for a hospital, but a temp agency pays you, who is your boss? Who are you responsible to? And importantly, as Jonathan Malesic asks in *The End of Burnout*, whose mission and values are you advancing?[43] Apple didn't have any part in my training, and we weren't tasked with upholding what they think a customer service experience should be like. Was I advancing Apple's values there? Should I have been? I didn't work for them.

Having a building filled with temps also means that your employees don't have upward mobility within the company; you can't work your way up from the mailroom to VP. You can't make the jump from maintenance to manufacturing, because you don't actually work there. Instead you're laid off and bounced to another mailroom at another company by your temp agency. Treating all of your workers like replaceable cogs, where you can just order another one, means

---

43 Jonathan Malesic, *The End of Burnout: Why Work Drains Us and How to Build Better Lives*, University of California Press, 2022.

they lose opportunities for advancement that they used to get from regular jobs.

Temp workers are a great deal for a company who wants to shift their risk onto their employees. When things would get busy, companies would hire temp workers from an agency. They'd show up, only when you needed them. They generally weren't paid as much as a regular employee, and the company didn't have to offer them any benefits. Best of all, when things got slow again, you could just tell them you didn't need them anymore. Permanent employees are expensive, and expect some kind of job security, but not temps. And not gig workers. *Sure, unstable and unpredictable work is harmful to employees, both financially and psychologically. But they're not real employees, so they aren't the company's problem.*

Corporations realized that they could save a lot of money by hiring temps or contract workers instead of regular employees, and that they could flex their workforce to meet their needs from one month to the next. They started firing their regular employees, only to hire them back as temps for the same job. It's also a tactic used to kill a union. You can't legally fire everyone and then hire back non-union employees, but you can absolutely lay everyone off and replace them with subcontractors to do the same work without benefits. Karen Ho, an anthropologist, says that the recent history of capitalism is unique in this way; the best interest of the company is now completely separated from the best interest of the employees.[44] Responsibility to your employees is seen as an obstacle to growth.

Deregulation means that legally, these companies may not owe us anything at all. Not security, or fairness, or quality of life. But morally, what do we owe each other?

Jonathan Severy shared an experience in Outside Online that he'd had with his neighbors, in the foothills of the Rocky Mountains. He was trail running, and a neighbor told him that he couldn't use a trail, it was private property. That if he saw him there again, he'd sue. Other

44 Petersen, *Can't Even.*

neighbors in the area had threatened more than just legal action. He didn't know if this actually was his neighbor's property, legally, but as he said, "Privilege and power ultimately determine what is a right."[45]

If your neighbor is pointing a gun at you, does it matter if the property is theirs? Something being legally correct is different from it being morally correct. We can take it upon ourselves to have a responsibility to treat each other well, even though the law doesn't compel us to do so. We need to accept personal responsibility for creating meaning and community in our lives. The same is true of our bosses, boards, and CEOs. Just because the law allows you to exploit someone doesn't make it right.

What responsibility do we have to each other? For each other? The downside to being rugged individualists is that it makes us risk averse, and self-preservation becomes our only instinct. *None of us owe each other anything, every man for himself.*

Treating people as entirely replaceable may lead to short-term gains, and this short-sightedness is entirely legal. Nobody is making you build your company on principles like fair wages for employees, job security, or benefits that allow your workers to keep themselves well.

They should be, but they aren't.

However, companies who are taking it upon themselves to be responsible to the people who make their business possible, who view their employees as assets and not expenses, are thriving. The best interest of a company, in the long view, is the best interest of its employees.

It Worked for Consultants

What led us to value being busy so much? Why do we view people with no boundaries between their work and their lives as virtuous,

45 Jonathan Severy, "This Trail Is Not Your Trail," OutsideOnline.com, May 9, 2020, outsideonline.com/culture/essays-culture/private-trails-neighboring-properties-dispute/.

as something to aspire to? Why have we prioritized work above everything else, even our health? How did this become the goal?

In 1948, Josef Pieper's work, *Leisure: the Basis of Culture* argued for a need to reclaim our dignity in a culture of overwork. Like the ancient Greeks, he saw our harried pace as self-destructive, and our commitment to constant work as a lack of commitment to accomplishing something of value.[46] We are profoundly, all-econompassingly busy, and yet so often feel that we haven't accomplished anything of merit. We are busy, even when we are not productive. So many hours of our day are wasted or go toward busywork that we wonder where our time has gone. Pieper wrote his manifesto in 1948, and our commitment to working as many hours as possible is stronger than ever. Why do we continue to work this way?

Well, a specific group of people were once rewarded for it. Elite consulting firms have run on a model of hiring ivy league students and then working them into the ground. If you didn't want to work 100-hour weeks, you were fired. If you weren't willing to sack employees with decades of loyalty to the company in the name of cutting costs, you were fired. Keep up or get out.

The cycle was so common, getting fired was sort of expected, and the workers would easily find new jobs with companies that they'd previously advised. Corporations started to fill up with these ex-consultants, and the ideology spread. Wall Street bankers still cling to an idea of constant work signaling eliteness and intelligence. Since they only took the best of the best, whatever schedule they came up with must be superior. If very intelligent people work too much, then working too much must be a sign that someone is very intelligent. Unlike many of us who also work too many hours, these bankers were rewarded with upward mobility, increased wages, and huge bonuses.

46 Maria Popova, "Leisure, the Basis of Culture: An Obscure German Philosopher's Timely 1948 Manifesto for Reclaiming Our Human Dignity in a Culture of Workaholism," *The Marginalian*, n.d., themarginalian.org/2015/08/10/leisure-the-basis-of-culture-josef-pieper/.

Historically, our middle class did get to experience a much smaller version of this. If the company did very well, you might get a raise or a bonus. These days, those profits only seem to flow upward. Maybe you'll get a pizza party. Consultants have set the standard to make everyone else work the way they do, but with far less compensation in exchange. Max Weber once said, "The Puritan wanted to work in a calling; we are forced to do so."[47] Consultants are the Puritans of the business world. Wall Street internalized these ideas—that good work is equated with overwork, and the idea spread to other corporations with them.

These workers—ideal workers—are expected to behave as though they have no other responsibilities. They've equated long hours of work with intelligence, but it's more likely a function of hiring young men who are only responsible for themselves. Ideal workers think only of work; they are always available.

Pieper describes the ideal worker a little differently in *Leisure*, as someone with a need to be part of a useful social organization who is ready to pointlessly suffer.[48] Ideal workers are machines. In fact, Jonathan Malesic writes in *The End of Burnout* that all of our work problems can be solved by the robot revolution—machines don't need autonomy or privacy. They don't need paychecks. They don't have dignity, or yearn for meaning. They have no families or communities or anything to get back home to.[49] Truly, the only problem they aren't able to solve is what to do with all the humans they'll displace. We've created a work culture that is best inhabited by robots, not humans.

Surely someone other than me has noticed by now that we are not actually being rewarded for giving all our hours to the company, by becoming work machines. Ideology like this is sticky, and hard to combat. Leaders who have made personal sacrifices to advance in their careers, who may have moved up in companies just like this, can have

47 Max Weber, *The Protestant Ethic and the Spirit of Capitalism* (New York: Simon and Schuster Digital, 2013), loc. 690, 794–795, 891, 1891–1894, 2160.

48 Pieper, *Leisure.*

49 Malesic, *The End of Burnout.*

trouble accepting that there are other ways to succeed, even when confronted with evidence of it. When they've succeeded in this kind of environment, where they basically live at work and are told what wonderful, devoted employees they are, they hold onto those values.

Consulting firms have given us the concept of the ideal worker, who devotes their entire life to the company. Even with piles of research showing how much time we waste, even without any tangible reward, we still *feel* like the way to get ahead is to be seen working. We still feel like every moment we spend not working, someone else is getting ahead of us. It doesn't really matter what we actually accomplish, as long as we show how devoted we are to work.

As a culture, we're not all that interested in what a person is doing, as long as they're always doing it. We've equated busy with productive, choosing quantity over quality, and glorified hustle over living a healthy, balanced life. Usually when you hear someone bragging about how many hours they're putting in, or how they only sleep three hours a night, they don't talk about what they're actually doing. What did they accomplish in those many many hours? *That's not important, because they were* doing.

Years ago, Fiverr ran ads that read, "You eat coffee for lunch. Sleep deprivation is your drug of choice. You might be a doer."[50] While many of us found the ads depressing, it remains a socially acceptable way to talk about work. Hustle culture values the doing, and isn't all that interested in why, exactly, you had to pull eighteen-hour days for months to make that launch happen.

We commit our lives to work, and because of this, our boundaries between work and life have become easily crossed. Our work follows us on vacation, and our life follows us to work. Boundaries between our work and our leisure have blurred, and it's largely by design. I remember when I first started seeing job listings that offered what

---

50 Ellen Scott, "People Are Not Pleased with Fiverr's Deeply Depressing Advert," December 12, 2019, metro.co.uk/2017/03/10/people-are-not-pleased-with-fiverrs-deeply-depressing-advert-6500359/.

seemed like fun perks—foosball tables, climbing walls, free food, cozy lounge spaces well appointed with snacks.

They aren't just perks. They are practices pulled straight from Wall Street. Organizational perks were standard there, and the point of them was to incentivize you to work longer hours. If work is more like home, why the rush to go home? Companies would let you order takeout and charge it to them, if you stayed at work past dinner. Since you're already here late, you may as well keep going until 9, when they'd let you take a black car home on their dime. They paid for these perks, but they meant more people working more billable hours.

Now that so many of us work remotely from anywhere, companies don't even have to pony up for snacks. We're even more capable of working all the time, and the hours we put in have become the only metric for success.

Hustle Culture Is Not Inevitable

So we find ourselves here. Our morality around work, the shifting of risks from companies to employees, and a few hundred years of historical and social developments have led us to our current burnout culture. The Fear drives us to maximize our productivity, and we're good at it, because work is such a big part of our identity. All of this can make it easy to think of hustle culture as just an inevitable by-product of work, of capitalism.

Of course we want to work harder! We want to make more money, we want to do work that is meaningful, a strong work ethic is simple human nature. But hustle culture isn't an inherent part of our existence, like gravity. It's something that we have collectively created.

Cultures can be formed by neglect or by choice, and they reward whatever attributes allow us to function as a society together. Our beliefs and our attitudes are grounded in an understanding of human nature, but our ideas about what is "simply human nature" have changed over time. Joyce Appleby writes in *The Relentless Revolution* that people in different eras have had vastly different ideas of the fundamental experience of being human—people have been viewed as self-interested, as rational, as sinful and beyond saving.[51] There is no consensus on what human nature is. Likewise, there is no one right answer to what a culture should be.

Maybe all people are self-interested, but what interests them largely depends on the society that they are a part of, the culture they exist within. Our current culture is interested in work. We are drowning in it. Three out of five people surveyed by the American Psychological Association's Work and Well Being Survey said that they've been impacted negatively by their work stress, citing things like physical and mental fatigue, lack of motivation, and general exhaustion.[52]

Sometimes, this work culture is built intentionally. While workplaces could avoid burning out their employees by hiring more people, or by changing either the amount of tasks or their timelines to suit their current workforce, many take the cheaper route of just squeezing more hours out of the employees who already work there.

Most people aren't all that motivated to work harder just to save a company, so the businesses really do have to sell it. They'll have to convince their employees that happiness is just on the other side of a total commitment to their work. They'll tell them that the project they're working on will change the world, that the work they're doing is important and meaningful. That they're making art, changing lives.

Here at Bad Time Management Inc., we hire our employees because of their passion, and aren't you passionate about your work? Don't you live for code, for design, for writing, for administrative busywork? Our company is a family, and our family needs you.

You hear this rationalizing so often, at so many different companies, that it's a struggle not to internalize it. And if you truly do love the work that you do, it's an even easier sell. Some companies

51 Appleby, *Relentless Revolution.*

52 Ashley Abramson, "Burnout and Stress Are Everywhere," *APA*, January 1, 2022, apa.org/monitor/2022/01/special-burnout-stress.

push presentism, where they reward those workers who are first in and last out, where crunch time is all the time.

I've worked many places where everything was an emergency, everything needed to be done yesterday, something was always on fire, and heroic overwork was the ethos. I am not a transplant surgeon, or a firefighter—none of the work that I do is of life or death importance. Once, I emailed my boss to let them know that I couldn't make it into work that day, because my father had suffered a heart attack (he's fine now), and they asked if I could still get some designs for billboards sent over. Reader, I could not. This kind of work culture is common, and it's led us to internalize that the only way we can further our careers is to always be working.

But not all work cultures are created intentionally. If you don't actively work toward a particular culture, one will simply form around you, and it may not be the one that you want. Perhaps it wasn't your intention to create a company culture where everyone is frazzled and exhausted, but you've allowed things to happen around you to contribute to it. You're not actively trying to stop it.

If you're willing to hop on a call at all hours, because it's 10am in London, then that becomes the norm. If your manager doesn't have time to get through her email at the office, and sends a response at 10pm, then *you* send a response to her response at 10:30, then that becomes what's expected. Because you're able to give something your immediate attention, you do, even though it could wait until morning. Without any specific policy to combat these intrusions into our off hours, we just sort of keep doing them, and companies find themselves creating a culture where everyone is always expected to be working, whether they intended for this to be the norm or not.

We haven't always felt this way about work. Society's attitudes about work have changed over and over again throughout history.

Aristocrats in the sixteenth century wouldn't celebrate our hustle culture. Thinking and talking about money was crass, and they honestly thought it was a little weird that merchants were so obsessed with it. It was their God-given right to be rich (some things, perhaps, haven't changed). Bragging about working a seventy-hour week would not have been something that raised your social standing at that time, because the culture then was different.

Malesic explains in *The End of Burnout* that long before that, in Aristotle's time, thought was the noblest pursuit. Labor was necessary, someone had to gather food and build shelter, but it wasn't noble. It wasn't virtuous.[53] Greek philosophers would be deeply unimpressed with your commitment to spreadsheets.

Historically, humans have considered their beliefs about how and why we work to be common sense. Popular beliefs like these come from the way that we interact with our world, our economic systems, our access to food and water, the way that we live and work within our corner of the world. When the way that our world works changes, those beliefs do, too. As Antonio Gramsci writes in his *Selections*, "common sense is a product of history."[54] It's driven by these popular beliefs, and often, it's wrong.

Before the eighteenth century, miasma theory was the common sense belief about disease transmission. Disease was caused by bad air, obviously. This was common sense, something that everyone believed. But eventually, we discovered microorganisms, and germ theory became the accepted scientific reason that we got sick.

Likewise, we now have so much research that shows the way we work is fighting against our own brains. We need downtime and rest and time away from our work to accomplish great things, and are instead asked to do the opposite.

We can see how the effort trap leads us to look only at the amount of hours we've put in, instead of looking at what we're actually producing, which devalues knowledge work. We can see how

53 Malesic, *The End of Burnout.*

54 Antonio Gramsci, *Selections from the Prison Notebooks of Antonio Gramsci* (International Publishers Company, 1989), 5083, 8338.

PART 2: HOW TO UNITE AGAINST BURNOUT

Chapter 3: Questions for a Burnout Revolution

So I've spent half a book detailing how we're being burned out and exploited, how our work culture makes our lives worse, and how many of us are doing this to ourselves.

Now, what are we going to do about it? Self-care isn't going to save us from our burnout, for that we need social change, and for *that* we need solidarity. We need to ask both how we can prevent our own burnout, and how we can prevent each other's.

Before we get there, we have a few more important questions to ask. Fighting burnout requires us to change the way that we view our work. For people who are immersed in hustle culture, it's a big mindset shift. We have to question if our moral framework around work and human dignity is correct, and whether we should feel compelled to be useful or productive. Are we only useful if our labor generates money? What exactly are we giving up to live this way? And who is benefiting from all this overwork?

Who Benefits from Our Overwork?

Who is burnout culture helping? Who benefits from all the long hours we're encouraged to put in? You probably won't be too surprised to hear that it isn't workers. Research shows over and over again that the best employees are healthy, happy, and well-rested. This is clearly at odds with hustle culture.

So if it's not us, it must be our bosses, right? Long hours must be necessary to get the work done, or they wouldn't insist on it. But overwork doesn't mean that employees are doing better work, just that they're doing more of it. For one thing, they're not using their time all that efficiently. If you know that you'll have to work ten or more hours in a day, what's the rush to get things done?

Even consultants, who have set the standard for hours of work being the one true metric, admit that a lot of that time is wasted. When the Harvard Business Review did a study at a consulting firm, they found that some employees were only claiming to work an eighty-hour week. Everyone reported that success at that firm required being the ideal worker, always on. But some of them found ways to work less, and just didn't mention it to anyone. Employees made deals with other coworkers to cover for each other, others took their work home with them so no one could see when they really clocked out. This makes it sound like they were just dodging their responsibilities, but they were all congratulated on the great work that they were doing. Apparently, they were able to complete all the work that mattered without putting in dozens of extra hours.[55] While secretly working a reasonable schedule, they still hit all the metrics that their company values. The extra hours were really just for show.

As a society, we're putting in a whole lot of hours for show. The average salaried workweek in the United States is 34.6 hours, but nearly 40% of US workers put in at least 50 hours a week, and 18% of us are working more than 60 according to Senator Bernie Sanders' remarks in a 2024 committee hearing.[56] Economists have something they refer to as a productivity cliff. Bob Sullivan's CNBC article states that employee output falls sharply once you've hit 50 hours, and after

55 Erin Reid, "Why Some Men Pretend to Work Eighty-Hour Weeks," *Harvard Business Review*, April 28, 2015, hbr.org/2015/04/why-some-men-pretend-to-work-80-hour-weeks.

56 "Prepared Remarks: Chairman Bernie Sanders Leads HELP Committee Hearing on a Thirty-Two-Hour Workweek," March 14, 2024, sanders.senate.gov/press-releases/prepared-remarks-chairman-bernie-sanders-leads-help-committee-hearing-on-a-32-hour-workweek/.

55, it falls straight off a cliff. This tracks with a Stanford University study done by John Pencavel, which found that when working less than 49 hours per week, variations in a worker's output are proportional to their hours—more time spent working meant an increase in output. But when they worked over 49 hours, that rise in output decreased. In fact, his study found working 70 hours a week didn't produce any more output than working 55 hours a week did.[57] None.

That means that 40% of us are absolutely wasting 10 or 20 hours every single week, up to 40 entire days every year. No wonder we're burned out.

Exhausted employees are more prone to mistakes and accidents, which can set your productivity into the negative, when you account for the time you'll now have to spend fixing those mistakes. So many companies create a cutthroat burnout culture, thinking it's the path to success. *If you put enough pressure on your employees, they'll simply have to perform better.* What research actually finds is that all that pressure comes at a cost.

According to OSHA, workplace stress is responsible for more than 120,000 deaths annually.[58] A study by the WHO (World Health Organization) and ILO (International Labour Organization) found that long working hours (55 or more per week) were associated with 735,194 deaths from ischemic heart disease and stroke.[59] This is literally killing us.

---

57 Bob Sullivan, "Memo to Work Martyrs: Long Hours Make You Less Productive," CNBC, January 26, 2015, cnbc.com/2015/01/26/working-more-than-50-hours-makes-you-less-productive.html.

58 "Workplace Stress: Overview," Occupational Safety and Health Administration, osha.gov/workplace-stress/.

59 Frank Pega, Bálint Náfrádi, Natalie C. Momen, Yuka Ujita, Kai N. Streicher, and Annette M. Prüss-Üstün, "Global, Regional, and National Burdens of Ischemic Heart Disease and Stroke Attributable to Exposure to Long Working Hours for 194 Countries, 2000–2016: A Systematic Analysis from the WHO/ILO Joint Estimates of the Work-Related Burden of Disease and Injury," *Environment International* 154 (2021), sciencedirect.com/science/article/pii/S0160412021002208.

Following the Wall Street model for short-term gains, these kinds of cutthroat environments that run on stress and fear can ensure engagement for a while. It's an adrenaline rush for some workers. But in the long-term, it leads to harm and disengagement. The Harvard Business Review finds that disengaged workers have higher absenteeism rates, more accidents and errors, and lower productivity. They also reported that employees prefer a workplace that supports their well-being, even over other benefits.[60] And well-being comes from a positive culture. Stress may make diamonds, but bread rises when you let it rest. Turns out, people are more like bread.

Overwork harms our health, and our boss' bottom line, while it also destroys our planet. David Graeber, author of *Bullshit Jobs*, writes in an article for Big Issue magazine that it isn't our pleasures that are harming the Earth, but our Puritanism.[61] Our feeling that we have to suffer to deserve any joy at all means that even if there isn't any work that actually needs to be done, we must find some work to do. Because we must always, always be laboring.

Graeber outlines how all this work is bad for our planet. We intentionally design things to break, so that people will have to pay to replace them, which he says is one of the main reasons that we have such high levels of industrial production. We have the ability to design things that don't break, but that isn't good for business. Aside from the fact that we're wasting resources and creating pollution, we're also creating pointless work. If we built a thing that lasted, we wouldn't then have to build its replacement.

But we have to work, so that we can afford to live, even if that work doesn't need to be done. And it isn't enough for a business to break even anymore—they're expected to show perpetual growth.

60 Emma Seppälä and Kim Cameron, "Proof That Positive Work Cultures Are More Productive," *Harvard Business Review*, December 1, 2015, hbr.org/2015/12/proof-that-positive-work-cultures-are-more-productive.

61 David Graeber, "David Graeber: 'To Save the World, We're Going to Have to Stop Working,'" *Big Issue*, September 8, 2020, bigissue.com/opinion/david-graeber-to-save-the-world-were-going-to-have-to-stop-working/.

Making a product that people love doesn't matter, you have to make more money, every single year, forever. So we labor in factories to make things that will break on purpose. Because the growth line goes up when we do. And many of us view our work not as a service, but as a means to an end.

This may sound like I don't believe that any work is worthwhile, and that's not the case. People do things that are of great value to humanity every day, but not all of those things generate value for shareholders. Whether people are pushed to build cogs we don't need for a paycheck or are building cogs that improve people's lives, we are all subject to a culture that tells us we should be spending more of our hours on work, even while research shows that it leads to worse outcomes for everyone.

Recent Hits to Labor

Something has to give. Hustle culture tells us that we should want to work all the time, out of love or drive, that we'll be rewarded for this devotion. But we know now that all of our long hours are producing worse outcomes, for us and our bosses. On top of that, work itself ain't what it used to be. Many pathways to careers aren't available anymore, and the way that creatives used to make a living are no longer an option.

Let's look at writing. Henry David Thoreau worked for much of his adult life at his family's pencil factory, but he rather famously moved to a tiny house in the woods for two years to focus on his writing. At the time, he was paid quite a lot more than writers are today; in fact writers are generally paid less now than they were 50 years ago. In a *Defector* article, Kelsey McKinney wrote that Ernest Hemingway was paid $1 per word for his articles in 1936, which adjusted for inflation would be around $21 per word today.[62]

62 Kelsey McKinney, "The Money Is in All the Wrong Places," *Defector*, August 10, 2022, defector.com/the-money-is-in-all-the-wrong-places.

Granted, Thoreau and Hemingway are both excellent writers, generational talents. But even excellent modern writers aren't paid anywhere close to this amount. Careers that were once available to writers and journalists, where you could build a life on a few well-researched articles in a month, no longer exist. This is the case for many different industries, where advice from someone who landed such a gig even thirty years ago is no longer remotely relevant.

When students fresh out of college ask me how to break into photography, I don't know what to tell them. Because the way that I built my career is no longer available to them. Some of this change is due to shifting risks—magazines that used to hire staff writers now have a loose collection of stringers who are working freelance for, probably, several publications. These are gigs now, not jobs, and certainly not careers.

Still, we do see wins when people are able to band together. The writer's guild of America went on strike in 2023 for 148 days, and SAG-AFTRA joined them. Studio executives basically said, "Let them starve," but they persisted and won regulations for the use of AI, minimum staffing requirements, and better residual payments. Though their strike ended, many of them continued to walk picket lines with SAG-AFTRA, who remained on strike until that November. Matthew Weiner, who you may know as the guy who created *Mad Men*, picketed alongside actors, telling AP News, "We would never have had the leverage we had if SAG had not gone out."[63] Solidarity gives us power.

There is often a feeling among the public, though, that those going on strike are simply ungrateful. They're writing a TV show for a living, that's basically a dream job, and they should be happy that they get paid at all. The same ideas about sacrificial labor that make us feel guilty about being paid to do work we enjoy can also make us feel guilty about asking for better treatment.

63 Andrew Dalton, "The Hollywood Writers Strike Is Over after Guild Leaders Approve Contract with Studios," *AP News*, September 26, 2023, apnews.com/article/writers-strike-deal-hollywood-vote-actors-d3119d670a4fd3449773bf8f4026fb2b.

For change to happen, it's important not to view ourselves as lucky to have "dream jobs," but as workers who are producing something valuable that companies use to make profits. Game Workers United campaigned to end "crunch," a term people in the industry use to describe their excessive unpaid overtime. Labor is still labor, even if that labor can be kind of fun, or interesting, or fulfilling. Artists and creatives make valuable work, and they're not ungrateful for wanting to be properly compensated and treated like a person. Especially as larger corporations *are* making money from your work. Working long hours for months isn't any better for you because the work you're doing is to produce a video game.

If the work is its own reward, there's a temptation to just feel grateful that you get to do it; it is the basis of sacrificial labor. But having work that is meaningful, even creative or exciting, doesn't pay the bills. Exposure and gratitude don't pay the bills. Creative fulfillment doesn't pay the bills. Industry giants are themselves making money with the things that you create, why does no one tell them they should just be grateful for the opportunity to work in a creative business?

If that work isn't valuable—it's just a drawing, or just a movie, or just some other beautiful thing that lacks utility—then how are they selling it for so much? When you're willing to give your work, your labor, away for pennies, just grateful for the opportunity to do it, how can you get to a place where you can demand any better?

We have to have solidarity with each other as artists, to say that this work is valuable, it is meaningful, and it is worthy of fair pay.

Do We Have to Be Useful?

Having work that is fulfilling and meaningful can seem like a privilege. I have personally been paid to draw, while there are people out there welding beams together to make buildings that other people live and work in. Their work is useful in a way that mine is not, but useful is not the only measure of worth in the world.

Our morality around work is centered on the idea of being useful, but do we have to be?

Things do not have to be useful to matter to us. Purpose is different from meaning. There are plenty of things in our lives that are good for humanity that most wouldn't describe as useful, and the growing demands of hustle culture mean that there's less room for them.

There's no space for contemplative thought when we are this busy. The artist, the poet, the musician, the writer, the philosopher all stand outside of what Pieper calls the "chain of efficiency" in *Leisure.* Their jobs are to step outside of our work world, to transcend it. To consider the wondrous and the astonishing, what Goethe calls the highest state that we can aspire to.[64]

But these things are not useful. You can't heat a home with them or feed a family or use them as transportation. They are not necessary for human survival. Station Eleven, a traveling symphony, has a motto: "survival is insufficient." Such is art, music, philosophy, leisure. Not useful, and yet essential. When we stop valuing things that lack utility, we make our world less beautiful.

We no longer put money toward the humanities, and we don't value the time put into it. We value getting the thing done as cheaply as possible before moving on to the next thing. We don't value someone learning to make things like stunning architecture and delicate cornices and sculptures that make the world more wondrous and astonishing. These things are not useful, but they are important. They have meaning.

Is it worthwhile to categorize everything that we do as being useful or useless? Is the only work of value the kind that generates money? There is a freedom in uselessness. Philosophy is useless, in that there isn't any direct way to profit from it. It's a goal itself, it is

64 Pieper, *Leisure.*

purpose. Hustle culture doesn't value anything that lacks an obvious use—really it doesn't value anything that doesn't generate money.

Most of us have tried to resolve this binary of work and play, leisure and not-leisure, usefulness and uselessness, by finding purposeful work. But purpose is not the same thing as meaning. David Steindl Rast, a Benedictine monk, explains in his book *Essential Writings* that work is driven by purpose, where play (or leisure) is driven by meaning.[65] We work towards a purpose, something of practical need and value. If your work is to build a chair, once the chair is built, your purpose is achieved. You stop working, and you're done.

Play doesn't have a purpose; it's driven only by meaning. You can keep playing hide and seek, or surfing, or rolling down a hill until you want to stop—there's no achievement to reach. As long as it's meaningful, you can keep on doing it. Frivolous, useless things can be incredibly important to us. Think about the things that have brought meaning into your life. How many of those moments were in the service of work?

It may seem strange to praise uselessness. But the more you look around, the more you'll see how much value is added to your life by things that don't have obvious utility. Music doesn't serve a purpose, but it has meaning. Playing with my kids is useless, but it enriches my life and theirs. We are not little machines doing tasks, we are humans building lives. Work cannot be our whole lives. There has to be some parts of us that aren't in the service of labor.

Josef Pieper began his book, *Leisure*, with a defense of this kind of uselessness. After the second World War, he said that Germany was in the midst of rebuilding their metaphorical house. Shouldn't every effort, every bit of energy and time, be directed to nothing

---

65 Maria Popova, "Why We Lost Leisure: David Steindl-Rast on Purposeful Work, Play, and How to Find Meaning in the Magnificent Superfluities of Life," *The Marginalian*, n.d., themarginalian.org/2014/12/22/david-steindl-rast-leisure-gratefulness/.

other than rebuilding that house? According to Pieper, no. Building a house meant more than just securing their survival, it meant putting their entire lives back in order. Building a life means more than simply staying alive, it means including things like art and play and poetry. It means doing things with purpose, but also things with meaning. Leisure and play are essential parts of the human experience. Survival is insufficient.

What Are We Giving Up to Work This Way?

It's worth considering what we're giving up to work the way that we do. We're not only giving up our time, we're giving up our peace. Because we've so internalized hustle culture, this idea that more work is always inherently better, that we should always be doing and always optimizing our doing, we're giving up the very idea of actually relaxing. We give ourselves no time to simply be, to enjoy a thing fully, because our leisure time is so limited we have to optimize it too.

It's rare that we are entirely present, enjoying a thing on its own. We're watching Netflix, but we're also scrolling through social media. We get a coffee from the really good place, but we'll drink it on the road. We're playing with our kids, but we're also just checking in on Teams for a second. We hurry simply because we're used to hurrying.

My toddler stopped on a walk to check out an ant, and I was just about to tell him we had to get going, when I realized that we didn't. Why am I rushing him? He doesn't have a 1pm meeting he has to get back to. Hurrying out of habit, rushing from one thing to the next, makes our downtime feel tiring instead of restorative. But when your downtime is so limited, you feel like there isn't time for anything off schedule.

I hadn't anticipated seeing a cool ant, so I didn't put that in the schedule. We can't even fully relax into our free time, instead feeling that we must optimize our leisure time the same way we do our workweek. Overscheduling our free time and filling our days with as many things as we can. Author Annie Dillard says, in her book *The*

Writing Life, "A schedule defends from chaos and whim . . . each day is the same, so you remember the series afterward as a blurred and powerful pattern."[66]

Personally, I could use a bit more whim in my life. A bit more time to look at cool ants. The things you fill your day with are, as they say, the things you fill your life with. What are we filling our days with? Does it look like the sort of life we'd hoped to live? Many of us find meaning in, or at least ascribe meaning to, the work that fills most of our time. Without it, what is left? Who are you as a person outside of your work? What do you want out of your life? What do you actually enjoy doing?

Technology hasn't necessarily made our lives easier, but it has certainly made the pace of our lives faster. As Brett Scott, self-described economic anthropologist, writes in his Substack *Altered States of Monetary Consciousness*, there is more to work than simply the time we spend doing it—the experience of, say, spending ten hours carving a wooden door frame is very different from jumping between a hundred emails, meetings, and tasks for even four hours.[67] The work we're doing is less physically laborious, but it is mentally taxing. Technology accelerates everything, which has ratcheted up the expectations for what we should accomplish in a day.

Decades ago, responding to correspondence could take awhile. A friend of mine who works for a cemetery loves poring over the remnants of these missives, imagining a less hectic workday. You'd read a letter from someone with a question, perhaps where a grave was located. Hunt down the physical ledger where that information was kept, and search manually until you find the person's name. Find the envelopes, write out a letter by hand, and perhaps walk over to the

---

66 Maria Popova, "How We Spend Our Days Is How We Spend Our Lives: Annie Dillard on Choosing Presence Over Productivity," *The Marginalian*, n.d., themarginalian.org/2013/06/07/annie-dillard-the-writing-life-1/.

67 Brett Scott, "Tech Doesn't Make our Lives Easier. It Makes Them Faster," *Altered States of Monetary Consciousness*, asomo.co/p/tech-doesnt-make-our-lives-easier/.

post office to send it on its way. Now, we have digital databases and email, and the same task takes maybe a few minutes, tops. We fill that time with more work.

Kurt Vonnegut, novelist, famously endorses going out to buy one single envelope at a time. He could buy a hundred envelopes, a thousand, and keep them handy in the closet. But in the process of going to buy that one envelope, he meets people. He sees a fire engine, a baby, he pets a dog. Who knows what he'll see? Vonnegut declares that we are here on Earth to fart around, that is our purpose. Speed and convenience are getting in the way of us farting around.

Technology has changed the way we spend our workdays and our downtime. We're expected to work a lot, and we're also expected to consume a lot, leaving most of us feeling stressed out and hectic. Because we can watch, read, or listen to just about anything, we are overwhelmed with choice. We're battered by decision fatigue. We do these things quickly, so that we can shove in more things. All this consumption crowds out the time where we could be creating, and it makes it hard for us to do deep work, when our attention is so shallow.

We have different ideas now about what is and isn't convenient, and the pace of our lives changes our expectations. I found myself annoyed that the Libby app didn't have the book that I wanted, even though a few years ago, I'd have had to physically go to the library or a bookstore to access that book. I was annoyed that I'd, what, wasted thirty seconds looking for it? That they didn't have every book I could want on this planet Earth, available immediately? Trying to jam more things, more work, more experiences into the same amount of time fragments our attention and it's eroding our patience.

The idea of a digital detox, of backing away from technology, is to unplug your nervous system from the information machine. You haven't gone looking for this information; it's just pushed at you. Turning off all of the notifications on my phone has been the best thing I have ever done for my attention. Resetting expectations about the pace you want your life to take, and bringing more intention to the content you put in front of your eyeballs, can help you to feel more in control of your life. Slowing down allows you to build back your patience and attention.

We make the most of every hour, saving so much time with our commitment to efficiency, but what are we saving it for? Mostly, more work. We rush through our days, showing up but not really being present. We're accustomed to compressing our time and working at a high intensity.

In some areas, this is beneficial. Like sprinting as a workout, or limiting meeting times so that people are more engaged. You have less time to accomplish something, so you're hyperaware of how you're using your time. But this ideology has spread to the rest of our lives, even our leisure time. There are things that simply deserve to live in the luxury of stretched-out time. These are things that shouldn't be compressed or rushed. Dinner with friends, unstructured family time, listening to music—these leisure activities should be free to take however long they take.

But now, we listen to podcasts on double speed. What are we saving this time for? To consume more things? I once watched a fellow violinist leave her phone on her music stand, and watch TikTok videos during rests. Not even super long ones, just a few measures. Filling every possible second with content. Books were once more expensive and harder to come by than they are now, and reading was a deeply engaged practice. People would read books aloud, would study them over time. Reading material is abundant now, which is wonderful, and so is every other form of entertainment that's vying for our attention. We take in information all day long, but it's often just a way to pass the time, not to be really present in it. The passage of time feels different when we're deeply engaged with something. Deep time, where we're truly present, can hardly feel like any time has passed at all.

As we fill every free moment with activity, each one feels like a means to an end. There's a drive to not just do a thing for fun, but to excel at it, and to then use it to make money. When I was pregnant with my youngest son, I learned to knit. I started doing it to make a stuffed bunny for him. It turned out beautifully, and my first thought after finishing it was, *I could sell this.* Even though I didn't urgently need the money from selling it. Even though I didn't really want to knit as a job. Even though being under pressure to create things by certain deadlines, to organize orders, to ship them, to argue with customers would suck out every ounce of joy I got from knitting. It was still my first thought, because we are so immersed in this culture.

Poverty of money and resources also means a poverty of time. We don't have time to explore new hobbies or new skills, because every hour is so valuable. We don't have time to do something for fun, because that time is for earning money. A devotion to work means that we can't putter around and try a thing, because we cannot afford for that time to be wasted.

But such wonderful things come from puttering. When we have time for reflection and contemplation, we feel more balanced and less anxious. We are happier when we see our friends, and when we volunteer to help.

This all seems intuitively true to us. The times in your life when you've felt peaceful and happy are likely also times when you didn't feel rushed. Leisure isn't just pleasant, it's foundational to our social ties.

But our schedules can make even the idea of planning a leisure activity feel like it requires too much energy. Being overworked means that we aren't spending our time with others, even though our lives are improved by it. There's the physical energy of doing the thing, the mental energy that goes into planning it, sometimes the actual monetary cost. It feels too hard, too tiring to spend real quality time with other people.

But what is a life without other people? If your life didn't feel so compressed, what might you choose to do with your free time? In theory, I'd love to take our little family on a weekend hike or a picnic. In practice, by the end of the week, I just want to disassociate in front of the TV.

There are larger dangers to reducing ourselves to our functions, our tasks, our social use. Our lives spin around work, and Pieper warns that this is causing a "spiritual narrowing." Some might even argue we're giving up our very humanity to work this way.

I belong to a few photography forums, as a way to connect with other people doing the kind of work that I do. One member posted to ask for advice. I'll call her Sarah. She'd paid someone else to take their family photos, but hadn't received them, even though it had been months. Sarah's photographer had posted, publicly, that they were suffering a major health crisis.

Sarah wanted to be sympathetic, but also wanted the photos that she'd paid for. The comment section was filled with people outlining the various terrible life events they had worked through. Deaths of parents, surgeries, losing a home to a fire, miscarriages, you name it—these people didn't miss a beat working right through them. Many said, "At the end of the day, it's business, and you gotta get your work done."

How are we so poisoned as a culture to think that's a normal way to view these things? Some things, some life events, mean that work stops. It is good and right that it stops. But somehow, we've all absorbed this idea that instead of surrounding ourselves with the love of our family, and taking time to process a life-altering event, the moral thing is to keep sending your little emails. *I know you lost your father, but three days is long enough, and these spreadsheets don't fill themselves out.*

We all, collectively, worked through an attempted coup in 2021. We're arguably working through an actual coup now, four years later. We continue to work while the world burns, sometimes very literally, and share articles about whether shorts are appropriate in the office when it's 110 degrees. There is no event so catastrophic that we won't just continue to reshape our lives to fit our work. In hustle culture, there is nothing that is more important than work. But work alone is not enough to build a meaningful life.

Why is it so hard to free ourselves from this need to schedule and optimize? And what is the constant onslaught of content and input doing to us? We've become so addicted to stimulation that some of us find the idea of being alone with our thoughts torturous. The University of Virginia conducted a study on this very thing, and found that many participants would rather subject themselves to electric shocks than to simply sit alone in their own company. In eleven studies, they found that participants in general didn't enjoy spending time (between six and fifteen minutes) in a room by themselves with nothing to do but think. They had a bad time.

Honestly, when was the last time you sat alone and did nothing but think for even six minutes? Not reading a book, or scrolling social media, or folding laundry, but just to sit and think? The ability to engage in conscious thought may be the defining thing that makes us human, and it turns out that people hate it.

These studies began by having people rate how enjoyable sitting in a room with no distractions was. They assigned some participants to entertain themselves with their own thoughts, and others with some kind of external activity, like reading or listening to music. People preferred having an activity to no activity. So, they wondered, would they rather have an unpleasant activity than no activity at all? For many of the participants, it turned out that being alone with their thoughts *was* an unpleasant activity.

Some of us actively avoid deep thought. We push away solitude and quiet contemplation, and fill our hours with work on purpose, so that we can avoid any self-introspection.

If you're busy, you don't have time to look at your life and consider if it's how you really want to live. You don't have to worry about deep thoughts, or big, difficult feelings. You don't have to confront imposter syndrome or loneliness. The researchers decided to offer the participants a different choice: entertain yourself with your thoughts, or administer an electric shock to yourself. As a treat. The study found that people would rather do something than nothing, even if that something is negative. 67% of the men in the study shocked themselves at least once, with one concerning outlier administering 190 shocks to himself. 25% of the women gave themselves a shock. What's especially wild is that earlier in the study, these same people had reported that they would pay money to avoid an electric shock.

Minds can be difficult to control, and it can be hard for some people to steer their thoughts in pleasant directions and keep them there. The University of Virginia's study found that humans prefer doing to thinking, even if what they're doing is so unpleasant they'd normally pay to avoid it.[68] We need the stimulation.

We've forgotten how to wait, to be. To let our minds wander. It's killing our creativity, and our quality of life. Every free moment that we have, in line at a store or at a red light, we fill with input. In neuroscientist Daniel Levitin's book, *The Organized Mind*, he says that information overload means we're buried in noise. Levitin wrote that in 2011, Americans consumed five times as much information as we did twenty-five years ago—outside of work, we're processing around one hundred thousand words every day.[69] We've rewired our neural patterns for distraction.

In uniting against burnout, we have to look not just at our work, but at our lives. Even once we recognize that no one benefits from our overwork—we don't, our bosses don't, even our planet is harmed by it—this ideology is hard to shake. Like we've rewired our brains for

---

68 Timothy D. Wilson, David A. Reinhard, Erin C. Westgate, Daniel T. Gilbert, Nicole Ellerbeck, Cheryl Hahn., Casey L. Brown, and Adi Shaked, "Social Psychology. Just Think: The Challenges of the Disengaged Mind," *Science* 345, no. 6192 (2014), 75–7, doi:10.1126/science.1250830/.

69 Derek Beres, "Being Busy Is Killing Our Ability to Think Creatively," *Big Think*, July 3, 2017, bigthink.com/neuropsych/creativity-and-distraction/.

distraction, we've built our mindset and our habits around this idea that we should be working all of the time.

Our devotion to work means that we're committed to optimizing our day for maximum efficiency, but this ethos has bled into every other aspect of our lives. We're modeling our free time around the way that we work, overscheduling ourselves and filling every second that we can with input and noise and content. We hurry through the things we're supposed to enjoy, because we hurry all of the time.

Many of us creative types feel grateful simply to have a job, to get paid anything at all to do what we love for a living, but this only makes us easier to exploit. We may feel that the work we do isn't useful, but useless things give great meaning to our lives.

Working until we're burned out, and living this way, means that we're giving up our peace, our ability to relax, and our time to socialize with others. We're putting work above all else when we should recognize that there are more important things in all our lives.

We are losing the things that make us human in the service of being our most efficient, and losing sight of what gives our lives meaning. All of these hours don't make for better work, just for more of it, more of our time spent away from the other things that matter. How much more are we willing to give up?

Chapter 4: How Do We Save Ourselves?

I've outlined here all the ways that hustle culture is hurting us, and yet hustle culture persists. This is the world we live in, and these are the things that our culture values. But we know that cultures can change, and that we can start with ourselves.

You've already taken a step toward that change, by reading about—and hopefully changing your own mindset about—how hustle culture devalues people, how our morality around work pushes us to burnout, and what your own parameters are for what makes a meaningful or successful life.

While many of the things that cause our burnout are society-wide issues, there are still things we can do to save ourselves from it, like embracing slowness, setting healthy boundaries, and truly caring for ourselves.

Opting Out

I'd like to start with something that all of us can do, regardless of our work cultures or financial situations, and that's to opt out of the hustle culture mindset. I'm not saying to opt out of hustle culture (although if you're able to, that's great for you.) Many of us aren't able to push back at work, or leave a bad culture, or change our workplace. But every one of us is in charge of what we believe about the world. Maybe Immanuel Kant believed that we can't trust anything that we didn't gain through suffering, but that doesn't mean that we have to.

Long hours may not be something you're able to escape, but you don't have to buy into the idea that it's the only way to be productive, or that being productive is the only way to be a good person. You decide what you value, and what success means to you. You can choose not to resign yourself to the idea that work is all you are. You can refuse to accept that shitty pay and bad conditions are what you get for doing work that you love, or the work that you can get.

You may yet have to accept the shitty pay, but at the least, you can stop believing that it's all you deserve. You can believe that the way things are isn't the way that they have to be forever—and that you shouldn't have to choose between doing a great job and thriving in your personal life. You can believe that each of us has dignity, entirely apart from our work. That our worth isn't decided by our productivity. You can believe these things, and no one can stop you.

You don't have to allow work into every tiny crevice of your life, or turn everything into an opportunity to optimize. You can resist the attention economy that takes away the small moments where you used to turn your brain off. You can just wait in line at the grocery store without checking your email "real quick." Instead of scrolling through every notification and reminder and beep and boop, you can opt to do things that ground you. To enjoy actual experiences. To seek a little solitude, where you're free from other people's input.

Jenny Odell, author of *How to Do Nothing*, writes that doing so can allow us to drop out of the "stream of productive time," to deepen our capacity for focus, connection, and curiosity.[70] In his Medium piece called *Rewilding Your Attention*, Clive Thompson outlines how our algorithmic feeds deliver us a kind of monotony, because they don't know us. They're made to reward what is recent and popular, which isn't an unreasonable thing to stay current about, but it's a very limited view of what is interesting. We contain multitudes, we are all

70 Jenny Odell, *How to Do Nothing: Resisting the Attention Economy* (Melville House, 2019).

of us more than one thing, and we are interested in more than one thing.

Thompson likens this to opening your social media app to see rows and rows of neatly planted corn—monocropping, when what we need is an intellectual forest.[71] He encourages us to rewild our attention, to make an active practice of embracing the weirdness. Being more intentional about what we consume, and how we interact with each other online, to allow more curious thoughts.

We can also use this social media time to form solidarity with each other, to support independent artists and media, to fight for improved conditions for all of us. You are the person who decides the best way for you to use social media; it's not something that you can do wrong.

You can decide not to martyr yourself for your job. To stop pushing yourself to do the absolute most at all times, to not make work your whole life. This used to be expected, that people would show up for their shift when it started, and go home when it ended. You may feel locked in to doing extra work just to keep your job, but you don't have to feel that they're right to demand it.

I started dealing with these expectations when I was in high school. One time, my English teacher called my mother. I was getting an A in the class, I turned in all of my work, and I did what was asked of me, but she was troubled that I wasn't enthusiastic about the class. I didn't seem happy enough to be there, apparently. But I was doing my job! Why should I also have to feign enthusiasm?

In the world of work, the consensus among managers is that this attitude—show up and do what is asked of you—might be okay for a job, but certainly not for a career. Careers are about paying dues, building something over the long-term, and that requires you to sacrifice. But are we being rewarded for all this sacrifice anymore? Perhaps people don't feel a sense of loyalty to their jobs because their

---

71 Clive Thompson, "Rewilding Your Attention," UX Collective, August 26, 2021, uxdesign.cc/rewilding-your-attention-d518ede18855.

employers show no loyalty to their employees. Why should we be expected to give up enormous chunks of our lives, knowing that we might never get to retire, that the thing we're told to sacrifice for is never going to happen?

What if we created a different value system around our labor? What if we want to work for places that see us as full humans, with lives outside of the office?

As productivity expectations go up and wages don't, the only real way to square things *is* to do less work. If they aren't going to pay us more, then perhaps we need to stop giving them all of our productivity. Most of us have no problem doing hard work when we feel respected and valued, when we feel that our work is meaningful. But we're expected to give up our days to work for someone who thinks we're selfish to want to spend time with our family. We're expected to create surplus profits that never, ever trickle down to us.

We're not trying to end the concept of work; there are things worth accomplishing in the world, and those things take effort and time. But we are trying to think about what a better future could look like. One where we consider not only what workers owe to their employers, but what employers owe to their workers.

On this journey, you can consider what a better relationship with work looks like to you, and seek out opportunities to work for someone who values you.

You can take the time to honor your body. To stop ignoring the signals it gives you when things are too much. To listen to what you actually need instead of glorifying working while those alarm bells go off. To believe that pushing yourself until you break isn't something to valorize.

I learned how important it is to take care of myself the hard way. How taking on more work and running myself into the ground to get it done can set me up for years of my life hooked up to IV poles, taking so many pills that I had to organize them in a tackle box. The second time that I got sick, when I really should have known better, and done better to respect my limits and take care of myself, I was sick for five years. Five years of IV antibiotics, constant pain, and ER visits.

I can't say that I caused all of that; I know that I didn't. But I did make it so much worse than it had to be, because I wouldn't slow down. I learned that these concessions in relationship with self-care—real self-care—had huge ramifications if I ignored my body's needs.

We can all stop powering through sixty-hour weeks while we brag about how little sleep we're getting, and instead consider the damage that we might be doing to ourselves.

You can value healthcare, childcare, *care.* You can value systems that support all of us, and stop valuing systems that drain and exploit us. You may not have a choice in the kind of work you're doing, or how much is expected of you. You have the job that you could get, and you need the money it provides you. What you can opt out of is believing that all this overwork is good and virtuous, and anything other than exploitative and performative.

Just like in any religion, you don't have to adhere to an ideology that doesn't feel true to you. If you're not able to opt out of the grind itself, because it's the only way that you can keep the lights on, at least you'll know that you aren't struggling because you're a failure, you're struggling because this system is intentionally stacked against you. And if you are in a position to opt out, to not take on more work simply because you technically have the time to do it, you can go ahead and not feel the tiniest bit bad about it.

You can believe that there is more to your life than your work. You can reexamine the role that work should play in your life and in your identity, to find ways to make the money that you need and live the life that you want without burning yourself out. You can reprioritize your life above your work.

While we don't always have much choice in whether we work or in how much we work, co-director of Harvard's Labor and

Worklife Program, Benjamin Sachs, told Outside Online that he sees change coming in the labor market.[72] During the Great Resignation, millions of workers quit. Corporations have seen major worker strikes. Employees at huge enterprises have seen walkouts. Displays of collective power have had real effects, and we have the ability to redefine what work-life balance means to us. What does it mean to live a meaningful life? What parts of our days are non-negotiable?

It's easy to look at a culture that posts "rise n' grind" memes and think that you're the one doing it wrong. Because you need basic things like food and sleep to function. Because you can recognize that you work more effectively when you're less anxious and have enough downtime. Because you know that you can't pull all-nighters, and instead schedule your work realistically, so that you have time to care for yourself. Our culture makes you think that you're the one doing it wrong.

But you can be successful and do it in a way that's healthy. You can build a life that allows time and space to take care of yourself. You can stop feeling guilty any time you aren't working. You can remember that you own your time.

We often fill our days with other people's responsibilities. We're distracted by the enormous list of things we should do, or could do, and we don't ask ourselves if we even want to be doing those things. If those things are even important to us.

You can choose to believe that rest is important. That overwork shows a failure in our priorities, our boundaries, even our self-respect. Overworking means ignoring what's really important to do what is simply urgent. Bertrand Russell disagreed that an efficient life was a life worth living, writing in *Education and the Good Life*, "What will be

72 Gloria Liu, "It's Easy to Find Work-Life Balance. Just Find the Meaning of Life," OutsideOnline.com, February 7, 2022, outsideonline.com/health/wellness/finding-work-life-balance-meaning/.

the good of the conquest of leisure and health, if no one remembers how to use them?"[73]

Maybe a successful life for you isn't terribly efficient. Being successful might mean living in a way that aligns with your values, or contributing to your community in ways that aren't monetary, or simply being happy. Maybe it's remembering the value of leisure and health. Success can look like a lot of different things, but you get to decide what it means to you. The people with the private jets telling you what success looks like don't have to live your life, you do. You get to build it the way that you want to. You don't have to measure your worth by your ability to perform, by how busy you are, by how much you get.

What success looks like to us, and what works for us, is something that can be reevaluated. It changed for me when I got sick, and then when I got sick again. It changed when I had my sons. I'd spent my whole career working two or three jobs at a time, and eventually realized that it meant any time I wasn't working, I was crashing to recover. All of my energy went to my job, and there was nothing left for the rest of my life, and there was no space for me to do what I needed to stay healthy.

So I stopped hustling. I rejected the idea that labor is central to my sense of self, and to my worth. I still work, but it's not all that I am. We can look at our lives, at our relationship to our kids, to our jobs, to our phones, and decide if this is how we want to live. We can refuse to blame ourselves for systemic problems, and also refuse to admit that we're powerless. We can opt out of this hustle culture ideology.

---

73 Maria Popova, "Why We Lost Leisure: David Steindl-Rast on Purposeful Work, Play, and How to Find Meaning in the Magnificent Superfluities of Life," *The Marginalian*, n.d., themarginalian.org/2014/12/22/david-steindl-rast-leisure-gratefulness/.

Living Slowly and the Cottagecore Movement

Our world is complex, and often, so is our work. It's difficult to process all of this complex information that we're bombarded with all day long when our schedules are so hectic, and that feeling of overwhelm contributes to our burnout. To make sense of our work, and to really experience our lives, we need to slow down and live with a bit more intention. To cultivate a sense of stillness.

Hustle culture values perpetual motion and growth. It calls for bigger, better, faster. But there are trends that show we as humans are finding ways to have that peace and stillness. The cottagecore trend developed through the 2010s, though it seems that Tumblr officially coined the term for it in 2018, according to Wikipedia[74] The images focus on a calm and quiet life, floral linens and clothes hung out on a clothesline in the sun. Woodland creatures abound. There's a garden, a cup of tea, stacks of books. It's not busy or productive; there's no hustle in cottagecore. Flowy dresses and peaceful flatlays of journals and fresh-baked bread dominate Instagram feeds, and it gives a sort of gauzy, romantic view of domestic labor.

People who have actually lived on working farms, or grown up in small cabins without modern amenities would likely have a very different view of what that life is like, and the cottagecore movement has also received criticism because tradwives who embrace it are glorifying regressive values.

But many modern homesteaders—who embrace the lifestyle of the cottagecore trend, not just the aesthetics—are radically trying to change the way that humans consume things, and they bring their progressive values with them. Kate Lindsay, writer of Embedded, interviewed some of the women who call themselves "radwives." They stress that you don't have to own land, or even move out to the country, or adopt a conservative worldview to embody the spirit of progressive homesteading. Instead, progressive homesteaders like Kathryn Laframboise say that all you really need to do is figure out

74 "Cottagecore," Wikipedia, n.d., en.wikipedia.org/wiki/cottagecore.

what community means to you, and explore what you're willing to do to uphold those values.[75]

Behind all the carefully curated cottagecore images is a lifestyle in contrast to the hustle culture we're immersed in and the modern ideal of having it all. It is mindful living and restful practices. Simple pleasures and small moments of joy. The idea of slowing down and moving toward a more rustic, community-based, and nature-focused life looks awfully appealing to those of us who feel chained to our laptops. Many of us find our lives too loud, too fast, too much, and have a desire to escape all that for a less frantic way of existing.

For some, even cottagecore tenets of slow living are not enough. They've embraced a more feral movement that they call goblincore. Where cottagecore romanticizes running away to a country life, goblincore romanticizes becoming a forest cryptid and living among the moss. Its aesthetic focuses on the less shiny parts of nature, like dirt and mushrooms—and crows that bring trinkets. It's gathering a little hoard of treasures. It is found or built, not bought. Unlike cottagecore, goblincore doesn't really aspire to anything presentable. It's letting yourself exist in whatever way you exist, without worrying about being presentable.

Maybe that all sounds silly to you. But these trends show a populace that wants to back away from the frantic pace of our lives. To enjoy small pleasures that feel attainable. Maybe I can't afford to vacation in the Maldives, but I can get joy from my little collection of weird rocks or feeding chickens in the yard. I can opt out of busyness as aesthetic, and gather my treasures in my comfortable, unpresentable clothes.

But even when we know it would be good for us, it's hard to take our foot off of the gas. We humans are hardwired for certain bad habits and compulsive behaviors. Brad Stulberg writes in his piece on being healthy in a dopamine-seeking culture that for most of our

75 Nick Catucci, "The Anti-Colonial Rad Wives of Instagram," *Embedded*, April 8, 2021, embedded.substack.com/p/the-anti-colonial-rad-wives-of-instagram.

history, we've lived in scarcity, where the best thing for us was to look for high-reward goods that didn't take a lot of energy. That meant that the easiest thing for us was also the best thing. But something that once helped a species can become a disadvantage, and in times of modern abundance, this approach drives us away from deep focus work and connection, and toward superficial distractions that are high-reward and require little energy.[76]

Deep focus work is a slower reward that requires a high level of effort. But everywhere we go, we are plagued by advertisements aimed right at the part of our brain that wants an immediate reward, showing us cool products and services that will fix all of our problems. The more that you're able to design your own environment to favor slow-reward activities—like deleting social media apps from your phone—the easier it becomes to ignore the siren call of easy fixes. The more time you spend doing deep focus activities, like reading this book, the easier it gets to choose them over the mental equivalent of junk food.

We're not driven only by our biology, but by our habits. Habits bypass your entire decision-making process, which is why researchers will tell you that people don't get more fit by willpower alone. When you have to make an active decision between putting on your running shoes and going back to bed, you're more likely to pick the immediate reward of those seven hundred thread count sheets. But when you rely on habit, you're more likely to do what you've always done.

When it comes to changing our lives and adopting a slower pace, the same thing is true. When you build a habit, you bypass the thinking, and go straight to The Thing We Do. This is something we can use to our benefit. In Charles Duhigg's book *The Power of Habit*, he describes how monkeys would start to crave juice after they received it as a reward for doing a task. If they didn't get their juice, they became angry and depressed. Researchers would try to distract

76 Brad Stulberg, "How to Be Healthy in a Dopamine-Seeking Culture," Outside-Online.com, July 17, 2024, outsideonline.com/health/wellness/health-dopamine-culture-evolutionary-mismatch.

them, by giving them other treats or time outside, but the monkeys would ignore them just for the chance that they might get juice.

Duhigg calls this a "habit loop." The monkeys get a cue (they get a task), launch a routine (they complete the task), and experience a reward (juice!). The cue creates anticipation for the reward, and it's the cue that creates the craving. That's the loop.

But you're not a monkey, right? You're a sophisticated person, not an animal driven by juice. When your computer chimes or your phone buzzes, your brain anticipates the distraction of opening an email. It probably won't even be a good email, and you know that, but there's a slim chance that it won't be spam. Maybe this time, it'll be juice. So you look forward to opening that email. To help overcome this habit loop, you have to eliminate the cue. If you disable the buzzing, the notification, then your habit loop no longer has a cue, and so you don't launch into your routine that reinforces the loop. You might go all day without even thinking about your email.

A few years ago, I turned off almost every notification on my phone. It only makes a sound at me now if I have an actual phone call, a text message, or a note in the app for my kid's preschool. Social media, games, and every other app on my phone is simply not allowed to notify me about anything. I'll check it when I damn well feel like it, and I'm not responding to pings all day long. I truly can't recommend it enough.

Changing your ideas about what is expected of you can help you to find joy and meaning. Giving the things in your life the time that they deserve to take can help you to live your life instead of just optimizing it.

We're used to having an outcome in mind for the things that we do, we're very goal-oriented. Which means that when we're cooking a meal, we often have a specific purpose in mind, counting calories and grams of protein. We're rarely making a meal just for the pleasure of eating. When we go for a walk, even if we don't have a destination in mind, we're trying to get in our ten thousand steps for the day, or to check off the "exercise" box. We aren't walking just to enjoy the walk.

But it can be beneficial for us to let go of the outcomes, to be present in the things that we are doing. Leonard Cohen once spoke to Pico Iyer for his book *The Art of Stillness*; Cohen told him that sitting still and listening to the crickets while at a monastery was the closest he'd come to real happiness.[77] But just as it isn't necessary to buy acres of land to live a slower life, you don't have to run off to a monastery to experience stillness. Honestly, who among us can afford to spend a month at a silent yoga retreat in the mountains? The austerity of your surroundings isn't the point, the contemplation is. We treat stillness, and leisure, as a luxury because we view time as a great luxury. But even a few minutes of mindfulness or meditative practice can make a difference in our lives.

Cottagecore is far from the first trend that has embraced the idea of slowing down. The slow cities movement encouraged walking over driving and choosing small shops over big chain stores and malls. Slow schooling questioned how we teach our children in a world that's so geared toward instant results, and reminded us that education is a slow process. These movements, and others like them, aren't against speed where it's appropriate; some things should go fast. Instead, they are against speed for its own sake, against the idea that speed is a virtue in itself. Or as Micah, @rincewind.run on Bluesky, very succinctly puts it, "Just because the clown car goes very fast does not mean it isn't full of clowns."[78] Speed is not synonymous with efficiency, success, quality, or importance. A slower approach is needed for many things, because it helps us to deal with the complex world that we live in.

---

77 Maria Popova, "Leonard Cohen and the Art of Stillness: Pico Iyer on What the Monastic Musician Taught Him about Presence," *The Marginalian*, n.d., themarginalian.org/2014/11/10/pico-iyer-the-art-of-stillness/.

78 Micah, @rincewind.run on Bluesky, bsky.app/profile/rincewind.run.

I've talked about how the collapse of a distinction between home and work has made us always accessible, how we can be reached anywhere at any time. But in addition to our constant accessibility, we also feel that we should respond immediately, simply because we can. In a cult of speed, delay is not acceptable. This expectation of immediate response means that there's less time for us to reflect or interpret. To reflect on something, to give it the thought that it likely deserves, requires some delay. In an increasingly complex world, more contemplation is required, not less.

A mindset of slowness allows us to more fully understand what it is that we're doing. After two decades of winging it, I started taking violin lessons. One thing I have really struggled with is learning to play fast passages with many notes—music that is complex. My teacher said that to learn to play something fast, you had to first play it very, very slowly.

This seemed counterintuitive to me, but my approach of trying to keep practicing it near tempo over and over was not working. My brain couldn't hang on to the information that I was trying to get it to memorize, because I was barely even clocking what a note was before I had to move on to the next, and I never played it through correctly. I could practice it that way a thousand times and see only the tiniest improvement. I wasn't playing it slowly enough to understand it.

When you slow down—enough that you can see what's coming next, that your brain can fully understand what it's doing—things stick. Coaches often advise their athletes to slow down their paces as a way to achieve faster race times. Slowing down on long runs allowed them to push more on their hard days, because their body could have a break. It also helped them to log more miles every week than they would have if they were going for top speed every time they went for a run. For athletes who are running long distances, racking up weekly miles is crucial.

Trainers also advise people not to speed through weight lifting, because it is much more important to focus on your form and do the movement well than it is to do it fast. Everything isn't about speed.

Slowing down and listening to your body can help you improve your endeavors, and it can also help you to build a sustainable practice. What good is it to run twenty miles one day if it means needing the next three weeks to recover? That's not a sustainable practice. When you aren't burning yourself out, you're more likely to stick to it.

This is a principle that extends way beyond exercise routines. Every year, I see people on the internet who are feeling too overwhelmed to do #inktober, a set of prompts that encourage you to draw something every day. I started my own daily drawing project this year, after doing one in 2014. But one change I'm making this year is to be a lot more flexible about it. The first time that I did a daily project, I would get very stressed out at the idea of missing a day, often staying up late to make sure that I finished it.

But I was the one putting that pressure on myself. I had given myself homework, and I was the only one grading it. This year, if I don't get my drawing finished for the day, I will catch up when I have time. If it takes a few days to catch up, then it does. The goal of this project, for me, is a sustainable drawing practice and a record of my time, not just checking off a box for the day.

A theme that you'll find throughout this book is that it is important to do things that feed our humanity without being in the service of work. Our leisure time cannot only be so that we're refreshed for work. Our self-care cannot be solely focused on getting us through the week.

We aren't looking for opportunities to slow down and be still because it improves our productivity in the long run, although it does. We fight against burnout by looking beyond the things that merely help us to tolerate our situation. We want to live, and thrive. It is important for all of us to find ways to slow down enough to actually experience our lives, and to find spots for joy in our days.

You don't have to upend your entire life to do it. You don't have to live off the grid, or take a vow of silence to reap the benefits of slowing down, or to live with more intention. We are driven by habits, and we can use that to our advantage by creating new habits that bring us a sense of peace.

Make time every day for something small and unplugged. It may be carving out time to really enjoy a meal, rather than scarfing down a burger in your car on the way to something else. It may be sitting around a table with friends, with no particular place to go. Lingering, instead of rushing to the next thing. It may be as small as having your coffee and not doing anything else—just that. Doing one thing at a time is remarkably calming. It helps you to cultivate focus, and to allow your brain to process complex thoughts.

You could take the time to read something long-form (you're doing it now!), or practice a new skill or hobby without considering the outcomes. You don't have to go full homesteader to find space in your life for slowness and intention. You just have to stop thinking that efficiency is the mark of a successful life.

Setting Boundaries

Opting out of a culture of overwork and an overly-optimized life means setting some boundaries. "Ideal workers" don't have boundaries. Healthy workers do.

There are a lot of ways to fight for boundaries, and how much you can afford to push back is definitely related to things like how much you need your current job, and how you think it'll be received. Speaking up, if you're able, is worth it. Making your needs explicit can change the culture of your workplace not just for you, but for everyone.

It's easy to say you should just quit a job, but maybe you're not in a position where you can do that, or maybe you just really like a lot of other aspects of your role and would rather stick around and try to improve things where you are. There are risks to rocking the boat at work, but setting healthy boundaries is a really important step in fighting burnout.

Work will take over all the other hours of your life if you let it. At one of the many places I've worked, everyone worked through lunch and ate at their desks. (Which was actually a bit of an improvement over working at the veterinary clinic, where nobody took a real lunch, and we didn't have desks, so I was often grabbing bits of a sandwich in between appointments or while I spun down blood.)

One day, a coworker said, "Hey, I'd like to take a walk. Anyone else wanna go?" And just like that, we became an office that went for lunch walks. It can seem like a workplace culture is immutable, but in some cases just a tiny push is all it takes to change it. Just one person speaking up, or showing others that they have needs outside of work.

So much of a culture is implicit, so to explicitly state your needs and concerns can really kick off changes in a workplace. It can help to normalize policy change for other people as well. When my husband was deciding how much leave to take after our son was born, he talked to other dads at his workplace who had taken leave. People who were public about it helped him to get a gauge of what his company was really okay with—which can be worlds apart from what's offered, or even what he was legally entitled to.

Taking more parental leave encourages others to take more leave, like actually using your vacation days encourages others to have a vacation, and opening up conversations about your needs encourages others to speak up. You pick up cues for what's acceptable from the people around you.

In addition to sparking changes, being vocal about boundaries also lets the people you work for know what really matters to you.

A Bright Horizons study found that fathers were more stressed about their work-life balance than they were about other issues that employers had thought were more important to them, like college savings and career advancements. So their study really found two things: that dads were stressed over work-life balance, and that their employers had no idea. They had assumed that other aspects of work were a higher priority to them, and they were wrong.

Your boss can't help you if they don't know that there's a problem. Employers have reported that they fear saying or doing the wrong thing, and so they often don't do anything when they see an employee struggling. They worry that they'll be invading your privacy, or making things worse for you, and so they simply stay out of it. But you can open up the conversation about your needs and focus it on solutions that will help you to do well.

It may seem incredibly obvious to you that, say, new dads would care about their work-life balance. Or that people want to be paid for the hours that they're working. Employers should know that! Yet sometimes, you still need to explicitly push back against policies if you want them to change.

While I was doing contract work for a university, I worked hours that I wasn't getting paid for. It wasn't just me—everyone on the team was doing work beyond what they were paid for, because that was the culture there. It was expected. But for my mental and physical wellbeing, not working off-the-clock was a boundary that I needed to set.

When you're setting a boundary, especially about something you've been allowing for weeks and that your workplace has come to expect, communication and managing expectations is important. I only worked part-time for them, twenty hours a week, so when I'd put in fifteen hours for the week, I would remind them that I only had five hours left. Often, they needed more work than they could afford, and they'd ask if I could maybe just do it anyway.

There's a temptation then to explain yourself. *Oh, I have this other project. I have another job, an appointment, some other scheduled thing that can't be moved.* But the best tip I've learned for saying no to something is to stop at no. Don't say, "No, I don't have a ride," because then the person will just offer you a ride, and you'll have to come up with some other reason why you can't do the thing. Say no, then stop talking. So I'd tell them, "I'm sorry, I only have twenty hours a week, and they've been used up."

I had always kept a time tracker, so I could even show them how long I spent on each aspect of the project, where all of those hours had gone. My boss wasn't excited about it; they were losing free labor. But she understood that I didn't want to work hours that I wasn't being paid for, that it's not an unreasonable demand.

I could have just kept my mouth shut, thinking they'd surely fire me if I made a fuss over something that everyone else at the company was doing. Instead, I stopped working for free, and so did the other people at the office. You don't always know how your company will react, and that's where setting boundaries can be hard. Even if they don't react poorly in an overt way, you might worry that they'll penalize you in other ways, either at work or socially, like by not inviting you out with the rest of the team. On the other hand, you may find that they're amenable to changes, and that you've been killing yourself to work inside parameters that other people don't require, or even care about at all.

At my very first internship, the bus schedule allowed me to either get to work half an hour early or five minutes late. So I showed up half an hour early. Months into it, I mentioned it in an offhand way to my supervisor who said, "Why didn't you say something? Just come in 5 minutes late. Who cares?" Speaking up has risks, but it can also have benefits, like getting to sleep in.

There's a lot of room between begrudgingly accepting a bad culture that's damaging your health and walking out with your middle finger in the air. There are degrees of rebellion. You may rebel in small ways, like being the person who suggests a lunch walk, and helping to normalize that practice.

Sometimes, we have to fight a bit harder than that. If you are in a position where you have some power, or even just the privilege of being the person who can set a boundary, you can change your workplace. You might set a precedent for not answering emails at midnight, or taking calls after hours.

If you're telecommuting or freelancing offsite, just setting work hours at all is a boundary many of us don't enforce. This is usually an implicit boundary that we set with our behavior, because we condition people on what availability to expect from us. When you immediately respond to an email at 9pm on a Sunday, you're telling people "I am fine with this. Please continue to send me things over the weekend and expect a response."

Sometimes even when we know that we need to set a boundary, we don't want to take the extra time and work to maintain them, because it can feel like you're fighting against the tide. But now that we can work from anywhere at any time, it's really important to set those boundaries, or we will work from everywhere all the time.

Many of us feel like we don't have the ability to do that, because it's the accepted culture in our workplace. *Everyone answers emails in their off hours.* But if you're in a position of actual authority where you work, know that your habits set the tone for your workplace. You have a lot of power in how you choose to work, and it sets the standard for how others are expected to work. You may be a night owl and answering emails late at night works for you, but remember you're setting that as the culture that's expected of the new parent in your office.

A client once failed to get our team the content that we needed to finish a project by the weekend as expected. They, of course, sent over that content at 4pm on a Friday, and I asked my boss if we'd need to come in on Saturday to get it done. He laughed, and said, "There's no such thing as a design emergency. We'll do it Monday." That's the culture that they've cultivated, through decisions like these.

Could we have worked late on Friday and come in on the weekend? Sure. Our client also could have gotten their content sent in by the deadline that we gave them. Poor planning on their part doesn't constitute an emergency on mine. You teach people how to treat you. If you go into crunch mode because the client missed their deadline, you're teaching them that it's fine if they miss their deadlines, the work will still get done. If you hold those boundaries, they learn that you mean them.

A concept that pervades hustle culture, especially for those who are running their own businesses, is that having boundaries around your work life is for losers. *Winners optimize every inch of their lives, and every hour is in service of work. Do you think Zuckerberg took a night off? We all have the same twenty-four hours, and look what they're doing with theirs! What's your excuse?*

For starters, we do not have the same twenty-four hours as Beyoncé. I mean, sure, we all have the same number of hours in a day, but we don't have the same amount of help. Beyoncé—and Taylor Swift, and Mark Cuban, and insert a bajillionaire's name here—has help that you likely do not. There are entire service industries that revolve around handling tasks, so Taylor Swift is not making her own lunch or sweeping her floors or folding her laundry. These people have nannies and assistants and drivers, which frees up quite a lot of their days.

Of course, this wasn't the case when they were starting their careers, unless they came from already wealthy families. Many of them will tell you that early in their careers, they worked from sunup to sundown, and that it's the secret to their success. Yet CEOs and founders who are reaping the rewards of building a huge empire contend that they still are putting in long hours and eschewing life balance, because the company is their life.

They love to share their schedules, to show how committed they are to their work, and as something for the rest of us to aspire to. Really, comparing any other person's schedule to yours, and taking their advice on how you should structure your days, is a pretty useless exercise. They are living a different life than you are.

Richard Branson reportedly wakes up at 5am, then spends 40 minutes lifting weights and the next 3 hours kitesurfing. I don't blame him. I'd probably spend my mornings kitesurfing too if that were an option for me. Billionaires all seem to wake up early, and they're very busy all day in vague ways, listed simply as "meetings" and "taking calls." But when they tell you that they're working fourteen-hour days, they're including the kitesurfing as part of that. Most of these schedules include the same few things in the morning—waking up early, meditation and exercise, planning their daily goals, a weird obsession with cold showers, and having a healthy breakfast. They include this as part of their workday, when tallying their hours.

Like Branson, I don't start working until 10am either, but I am definitely sleeping at 5am. My morning is mostly taken up by dragging myself out of bed at 7:45am or so, getting the kids ready and off to school, then having some coffee and, hopefully, something resembling a breakfast. That generally takes until around 10am. I feel it would be disingenuous to count any of this as part of my workday, but it's common for people to inflate the number of hours they're "working" in a day because overwork is seen as something to be praised. When the admission that you're putting in sixteen-hour days gets you a breathless writeup in *Wired*, you'll use whatever you can to pad that timesheet.

Most of us aren't getting interviewed by business magazines, and have hours of our own days that are taken up by tasks that billionaires no longer have to worry about. Personally, I have about six and a half hours every weekday where I'm not responsible for any kind of childcare (barring holidays, school closures, illness, or regular medical appointments). I do sometimes put in a few hours on evenings or weekends, but I don't make a habit of it. My evenings are generally spent making dinner, finding bookbags and shoes for the next day, and spending time with my family.

I'm positive that hustle culture proponents could make my schedule more efficient. They'd say I spend entirely too much of my time resting (chronic illness be damned, time is money). They'd say that I could take a working lunch, that I could fit in more hours during the evening or on weekends, maybe pay for more childcare so that more of my time can be spent on work.

But I would tell those people to kick rocks. Our current situation works for us. Everyone is fed, and the lights stay on. My husband works full-time, and that gives us health insurance. I don't have Mark Cuban money, but I have enough. My schedule works for the life that we have right now, which is always subject to change. One day I may need to make more time for work, but I have no interest in optimizing every second of my life for maximum productivity. I don't really believe that's the only way to have success in your life, and if it is, well, the price is too steep for me.

I talked about my own schedule here, not because I think it's a good schedule for you to try to adopt. It isn't. It's super specific to my life, my health, my family, my business, and the odds that it will help you achieve your own personal goals are pretty slim. It is just how I arrange my time right now—these are the boundaries I've set around the amount of hours I'm willing and able to devote to work.

Your schedule might allow time for reading, or baking, or gardening. You may do care work all day. You may wake up at noon. I don't live your life. Your schedule is yours, and if waking up at 5am doesn't fit in with your goals, there's no reason you should feel like you have to. You get to decide how much is enough. Your goals are your goals, and they can be wildly different from anyone else's. Your life can be wildly different from anyone else's. Hustle culture offers you one way to live a life, but there are infinite ways to do it. You can not only opt out of an overly-scheduled existence, you can also refuse to feel bad about it. Because there is no one-size-fits-all way to build a life.

This is another difficulty that we face in fighting hustle culture, though. Many of us still believe deep down that it's the one true way to success. That work has to be the way that work is. That we struggle to finish the work as it is now, how could we possibly work less?

But the fact is, there is always more work to be done, you can always find something else to do. *If you have time to lean, you have time to clean.* It's easy to find yourself still at the office two hours after closing time, working on something that could have waited until tomorrow. The fix for this isn't to just keep working every second of every day until you've finished something, it's to give yourself permission to call it a day.

When you ask yourself what it is that you need to feel finished for the day, the answer can't be "doing everything that needs doing." Work is finished when its purpose is fulfilled, when you've made a chair you are done making that chair. But there will always be another chair to make, another email, another tweak to that layout. Fixating on the endlessness of it, on how much there is still to do, keeps you from feeling any satisfaction for the things that you have done.

Changing our perspective from what needs to be done to what we can reasonably accomplish given our particular set of limitations can bring us peace. I may have nine hours worth of things that need to be done, but I only have these six and a half hours to work.

If you think that's an awfully short workday, there is a monastery in New Mexico where they limit their work to three or four hours a day. The monks' purpose is to pray, and that is what they spend the majority of their day doing, but they also do some work. When their three or four hours are up, they stop. If they have more that needs to be done, they stop anyway. For them, absolutely nothing takes precedence over the things they consider non-negotiable—time in prayer and gathering with their fellow monks.

When I say that I have nine hours of work that needs to be done, our common sentiment would be that I had best find the time to do it. To fit my life around my work, instead of my work around my life. A monastic life may be too extreme a fix for that, but perhaps we should be less willing to give up our own non-negotiables.

Much of what I've written here centers around changing what we value. That we should value having healthy boundaries, and balance between our work and our lives. That we can value other ways to live a life, that a life can have meaning independent of its productivity. It's also important for us to believe that we can change some of these values by speaking up about what matters to us, and to show those values through leadership.

Sometimes the hardest part is really believing that things can change. Mohammed Yunus, Nobel Peace Prize winning economist, said in his acceptance speech that one of the underpinnings of poverty is the idea that it's an ineradicable evil.[79] *We have always had poverty, therefore we will always have poverty.* How different could our society be if we believed, truly and deeply, that poverty is unacceptable? Would we have changed the policies that allow it, or built the institutions needed to eradicate it? As Ursula K. LeGuin, science fiction author, said in an acceptance speech of her own, "We live in capitalism, its power seems inescapable—but then, so did the divine right of kings."

The first step may be admitting that there's a problem, but an equally important step is believing that something can be done about it. That belief drives change.

Actual Self-Care

You may be surprised to find a chapter about self-care in a book called *Self-Care Won't Save Us.* While it isn't enough on its own, self-care does have a place in our fight against burnout. We often get so mired in our workweek that we don't prioritize our own basic care, or consider what that means for our health. We feel selfish or indulgent

79 Appleby, *Relentless Revolution.*

in taking time for ourselves, but we are mortal beings and we require some upkeep.

Self-care can take a lot of forms. It might mean filtering your social media feed to avoid things that raise your anxiety levels but don't offer any real benefit. It can mean taking a mental health day, or meditating. It might be asking for help, whether that's from friends or in more formal ways like taking medical leave. Or setting boundaries that are healthy for you. We are whole people with needs—food, water, rest, joy—and we ignore those needs at our own peril. As the saying goes, choose a day to rest or your body will choose one for you.

Self-care is also complicated by the fact that it's an $11 billion dollar industry that often leads to its own set of unrealistic expectations, as Anne Helen Petersen points out in her Buzzfeed article on burnout.[80] This consumer-driven incarnation of self-care sells us on little treats, like spa days or fancy candles or a seven-step skincare routine. These things feel nice, and maybe they do lift the fatigue we experience around our work lives a bit, but they aren't getting to the heart of what we really need. Of course, the wellness industry trying to make a buck off of overworked people goes back centuries. The Science Museum of London lists treatments for neurasthenia that included tonics and elixirs to buy, as well as therapy via electrified belts.[81] These days, we're pushing unregulated supplements and infrared face masks, but the core concept is the same—spend your way to better mental health. Corporations get richer, and your work reality remains just as distant from your expectations as it was before.

Workplaces are increasingly offering wellness programs to their employees, although many fall victim to these same problems that plague the consumer self-care industry. A recent study by researchers from Harvard Medical School and the University of Chicago that

---

80 Anne Helen Petersen, "How Millennials Became The Burnout Generation," *Buzzfeed*, buzzfeednews.com/article/annehelenpetersen/millennials-burnout-generation-debt-work.

81 "From Nerves to Neuroses," *Science Museum*, June 12, 2019, sciencemuseum.org.uk/objects-and-stories/medicine/nerves-neuroses.

focused on more than thirty thousand employees at a warehouse found that workers with access to wellness programs didn't really see much difference in absenteeism or job performance than those who didn't.[82] Another study by the National Bureau of Economic Research suggested that these kinds of programs don't really make employees healthier, but merely highlight the employees who already are healthy. And they can alienate those who aren't.

When my own workplace started focusing on physical health as team building exercises, most of my thoughts were focused on how to push through them without entirely embarrassing myself in front of new colleagues. These programs are often optional, but who wants to be seen as opting out of team building?

These programs can sometimes have a shiny veneer of health and wellness but fail at actually giving their employees what they need. Lauren, a former chef, reported to the Harvard Business Review that "The only job I've ever had that promoted wellness treated me the worst when I was at my least well." The retreat center where she'd worked offered their employees free access to a gym, discounts on spa treatments, sessions with a nutritionist, and catered meals. It all sounds pretty great, but mental health leave of any length was not included. So when Lauren was hospitalized for three weeks, as a complication of her bipolar disorder, she was fired.[83] She needed real care, but they only offered perks.

A true wellness program would focus on policies that allow you to be fully human, and humans sometimes need to step away from work. They sometimes need to alter their work schedules. Even self-care is framed not as a way for you to be actually well, but as a way to help you continue working. But just as leisure can't be solely for the sake

82 Zirui Song and Katherine Baicker, "Effect of a Workplace Wellness Program on Employee Health and Economic Outcomes: A Randomized Clinical Trial," *JAMA* 321, no. 15 (2019), doi.org/10.1001/jama.2019.3307.

83 Charlotte Lieberman, "What Wellness Programs Don't Do for Workers," *Harvard Business Review*, August 14, 2019, hbr.org/2019/08/what-wellness-programs-dont-do-for-workers.

of work, self-care can't either. As Charlotte Lieberman writes in that same Harvard Business Review article, wellness perks can't just be bribes to make up for an environment dedicated to overwork. Wellness programs have to be for the benefit of the employee, not the company. What seems to help employees to perform well are environments that are flexible about when and where people are allowed to work, so that they can adapt to whatever else is going on in their lives.[84]

When we're overwhelmed and stressed out, we tend to let the things that are easiest to overlook slip. Self-care is something that's easy for us to overlook. We leave ourselves as the last, lowest priority, and we suffer for it.

We all think that the worst simply can't happen to us, but putting off the things most important to our health can be literally deadly. A woman in Indonesia worked herself to death, tweeting the whole time about how hard she was hustling, as reported by Adweek and Medical Daily. A lack of sleep combined with too many energy drinks to stay awake killed her. At the root of it, a commitment to work above everything else in her life killed her. It's an extreme example, and most of us are more likely to suffer from burnout and declining mental health. But she's also not the only person this has ever happened to.

Taking care of your brain and your body is essential. Your work can be a big part of who you are, but it's still only a part. And it's something that you can't do at all if you aren't caring for yourself. Your body is not the enemy; it's working hard to support all these other things you want to do. It deserves a little compassion from you. Give your brain and body the resources they need to support your work, and your life. We think that we don't have time for it, we'll get to it later when things slow down. But our immune system gets wrecked by bad diets, not enough sleep, and too much work. Eventually, it'll give, and you'll spend more time being sick than if you'd just blocked out the time for self-care in the first place.

---

84 Ibid

When my son was very young, he wanted to sit with me. Not for all that long, maybe ten minutes, he just wanted to relax and be near me. It's a small request, just like remembering to eat lunch or go to bed at a reasonable hour are small requests. I learned early on that I could either give him what he needed, this small concession that helps him get through his day being a tiny person in a world that was still pretty new to him, or we could all suffer the consequences. I could try to keep writing, or doing the dishes, or whatever I was in the middle of while he'd cling to my legs. I'd be stressed, because he was upset. He'd be stressed, because he wasn't getting what he needed. We were all having a bad time.

Because instead of giving him the measly ten minutes that he needed, I'd spend twice as long muddling through a task while my blood pressure crept ever higher, only to end up sitting down with him anyway to get us both back to a calm and happy place. Which is what he wanted to do in the first place. This is how self-care works. If you skip lunch to keep working, then you end up sleepy and hangry. If you push your bedtime into the wee hours, you're dragging the whole next day, because coffee is not enough to make up for sleep deprivation. You're much less productive than if you'd just taken the time to do what your body needs.

You can finish most any task faster, more effectively, and more happily if you keep yourself in good condition to perform it. Which you already know how to do. You know what's best for you, you know how to do it, and so you have to make the time to do it. I didn't say "find the time," because you so rarely just stumble upon a pocket of free time. You're making decisions about how you spend your days. We either want to work or we have to work, and either way, this becomes a matter of making time to both do that work and care for yourself. I know this, because at one point I was only making the time for one of those.

When I got very sick during graduate school, I kept up appearances, and refused to admit that I needed more rest than my friends did. That I couldn't pull all-nighters, or live off of Doritos tacos and soda and still be a functional person. I'd been repeating a cycle of pushing myself too hard, then crashing. I didn't ask for help, and most of the people around me had no idea that I was sick.

But eventually I got on a treatment plan that worked, and I got better, and I learned absolutely nothing. I took that as an opportunity to work nonstop. I had a full-time job and also ran my own photography business. I was easily pulling sixty to eighty hours a week, because I'd spend my entire weekend and many evenings working. I was always working. I had to set alarms to remind myself to eat lunch, because I regularly worked through them.

The hours have to come from somewhere, so I wasn't getting enough sleep or exercise. I wasn't eating well. I wasn't resting, or doing any of the things that keep my immune system from singing "Take This Job and Shove It" on its way out the door. Less than a year later, I was sick again. In fact, I was much sicker than I'd been the first time around. Because I had to see a specialist, and I live very far away from him, starting treatment again meant a five-hour round trip to see the doctor at least once a month, and my sick leave didn't accrue quickly enough to cover it. I wasn't able to keep my illness from the people that I worked with anymore, and I ended up filing for FLMA to cover the time that I had to take off. This is the part where I finally started to take self-care seriously.

Taking the time to protect your health is worth taking seriously.

What changes can you make to the way you're caring, or not caring, for yourself? How can you fight against burnout?

For one thing, you can take your burnout seriously, and start to cope with it early, instead of waiting until it's an all-consuming problem. Take intentional breaks, like stepping away during lunch and adding mental downtime to your regular schedule, and take off longer blocks of time when you're able to. Lack of control is a main driver of burnout, so advocating for yourself at work can not only let your boss and colleagues know how you feel, but it can also restore your sense of agency at work.

You can set clear boundaries to keep work from creeping into your downtime. You can do things with your weekends that aren't work, to give yourself real time away from it. When you feel burned out, but have to continue working anyway, some experts recommend going into low power mode. Do what you absolutely need to do, and knock off tasks from your list that aren't essential. And give yourself time. A 2021 research study by Aarhus University in Denmark found that for those experiencing shorter term work stress, it took six to twelve weeks to recover, whereas those with more prolonged burnout could take longer than a year to fully recover.[85]

You can learn something from all of my mistakes and lean on your community for support—let your friends and family help you. Burnout often drives people to isolate themselves when they need others the most. You can limit things that drain your battery, like doomscrolling, and make time for things that energize you, like a journaling practice, time in nature, or mindfulness. Some of these things will resonate with you more than others, and it's up to you to decide what you need. But all of us have to prioritize necessary care, to practice compassion for ourselves, and to value giving ourselves the care and rest that we need to thrive.

We often say that rest is resistance. But writer Trey Washington argues in his article for Scalawag that this is shifting the risk and the burden away from the institutions that continue to steal our time and energy, putting them on us as individuals. Rest should not be a luxury that most of us can't afford, and the reasons it continues to feel like a luxury are systemic.

---

85 Arno van Dam, "A Clinical Perspective on Burnout: Diagnosis, Classification, and Treatment of Clinical Burnout," *European Journal of Work and Organizational Psychology* 30, no. 5 (2021), tandfonline.com/doi/full/10.1080/1359432X.2021.1948400?src=recsys.

I do still believe that taking the time to rest shows resistance to a culture that tells us it isn't important, and that it can be a way to push back on the boundaries that our work perpetually oversteps. But Washington makes a point in his article "Rest Is Not Resistance, and That Is Ok," that rest is not just a tool of resistance, but also an outcome. That we shouldn't give up our pursuit of rest, but that we must "merge it with responsibility."[86] Self-care is something that allows us to keep doing the work of mutual aid, fighting for a better social safety net and collective leverage, but it is also the thing we're responsible for fighting *for*.

We want everyone to have the option to opt out of work patterns that are harmful. To embrace a slow life if they choose, and to set boundaries around their work that allow balance in their lives. We can't do that with consumerism, or with wellness programs that only pay lip service to being well. For all of us to have the time and resources to care for ourselves, we have to care for each other. Saving ourselves is inextricably linked to saving each other.

86 Trey Washington, "Rest Is Not Resistance, and That Is OK," *Scalawag*, March 28, 2024, scalawagmagazine.org/2024/03/rest-is-not-resistance-and-that-is-ok/.

Chapter 5: How Do We Save Each Other?

We Need Leisure for Solidarity, We Need Solidarity for Change

Self-care is not enough to save any of us from burnout. We can explore other ways of working, like four-day workweeks and cooperative models, but the most important thing that we need to achieve real change is solidarity with each other. And for that, we need leisure.

Leisure is an important part of real, true self-care. We develop our sense of self and our place in the world in downtime. But our culture doesn't value leisure, perhaps because we don't really understand its purpose. For many of us, even the suggestion that we should value leisure sounds bizarre.

We value productivity, accomplishment, and work ethic. We value putting in many, many hours toward those goals. But rest? Relaxation? Fun? These aren't viewed as good or valuable things. They're self-indulgent, lazy, even.

Many of us have lost sight of what we even feel like doing, what we do just for our own joy. Ask any parent who has an unexpected break in their childcare duties; we can feel a little lost as to what to do with that time. But the truth is that many of humanity's greatest achievements weren't made in constant hectic hustle. They were made in downtime, in solitude with our own thoughts.

Leisure is not indulgent, but a necessary part of being a human. The root word for leisure, *licere* in Latin, means "to be free." Leisure is time that you should be free, and it is both freedom for and freedom from. Freedom for doing what you feel like, and freedom from the need to generate value.

It's hard to say how much time we actually spend at leisure, because time diaries are self-reported. Also, some sociologists have historically categorized childcare as leisure, and those sociologists absolutely do not have children. What we do know is that we all pick up cues from the culture around us about how to live our lives. We may not intentionally choose hustle culture, but if we're surrounded by people who are always in a hurry, then we will be hurried too.

We don't consider our downtime to be important, yet the most significant human achievements have been made through leisure. In March of 1905, Albert Einstein submitted a paper that challenged the consensus that light was a wave, insisting instead that it was a particle. (You might have heard of it.) In May, he submitted another paper challenging the belief that atoms didn't exist, with proof that they did. In June, a third paper, proposing that time and space were the same, his infamous theory of relativity. In September, one more paper as a follow-up to support that theory. 1905 was known as Einstein's miracle year. By the end of his career, he'd published more than three hundred such papers, won the Nobel Prize in physics, and became the go-to example for the rest of time when you want to call someone a genius. How did he do it all? He made time for solitude, for deep thought.

These days, we have different expectations of ourselves, and they're arguably pretty unrealistic. Answer every email, keep a clean house, exercise, be a supermom, go to bed on time, excel in our careers, care for our elders, read about current events, run our children to various life-enriching activities, keep up with all the latest productivity tips and hacks and gadgets, plus there's our actual jobs, which we insist on putting in more and more hours every week for.

We are busy. We can't relax, because we feel guilty about relaxing, because doing nothing is for lazy people.

I hate to break it to you, but Einstein was lazy people. In his defense, science fiction writer Robert Heinlein has famously written in his book *Time Enough for Love* that progress is made by "lazy men, trying to find easier ways to do something." They work smarter, not harder.

Solitude allows us to discover solutions, to get clarity to make better decisions. When we're doing nothing, physically, our brains are still doing something. Sitting alone with our thoughts gives us the time to explore new ideas. Einstein went for long walks, or to spend time in quiet cabins, or to sail on his boat so that he could have time alone to think. Just think. No correspondence, visits, or meetings. No email. He allowed himself downtime to think deeply.

Solitude doesn't have to require physical space, but it does require a lack of input from others. We have to shut out the external noise of the world. This kind of solitude is conducive to thought, the kind of really deep thought that sometimes ends with Nobel Prizes. Finland's tourist board put out a series of photos that featured a solitary person in the wilderness, with the caption "Silence, please." They marketed the quiet as a draw for tourists. It's something that can be hard to come by for many of us.

We live in a fairly rural area, but our house is surrounded on three sides by different modes of transportation—trains, cars, and barges on the river. It's rarely all that quiet, even here, and it's worse for city dwellers. Epidemiologists have found a correlation between a number of health problems, including high blood pressure, loss of sleep, heart disease, and tinnitus, with chronically noisy environments.

Noise activates the amygdala, which prompts the body to release cortisol. Constant noise can mean constantly elevated cortisol. No wonder there's such a huge market for noise canceling headphones. Imke Kirste, a regenerative biologist at Duke University, tested various sounds and silence on mice. The silence was meant to be a control, so it wasn't expected to produce any interesting results. It's silence, non-input—what could it do to the brain?

It turned out that the absence of input had a bigger effect on their brains than any of the input they tested. Two hours of silence every day led to the mice creating new cells that became working neurons. Kirste's working theory is that the silence was such a huge contrast to the mice's usual noisy environments that it led to the mice being more sensitive, more alert. Like when your children are playing in another room, and you suddenly realize that they've been very, very quiet, putting you on high alert. Kirste did stress that these results are preliminary, and have not been replicated in humans.[87] Silence may not lead to neurogenesis in people, but it is powerful.

Many of our great historical thinkers sought solitude, because it really is effective. It improves not just our productivity, but our creativity and decision-making. Einstein's solitary days on a sailboat allowed him a great deal of calm and quiet time, with his own thoughts. Lin-Manuel Miranda came up with the idea for *Hamilton* while he was on vacation. Galileo made discoveries that would one day lead to your smart watch by observing a pendulum swinging in a cathedral. Oliver Sacks came up with a theory about how music affects our brain while hiking through Norway.

I often take a walk when I feel stuck on a creative task, and I know I'm not alone. Time spent at leisure, and time spent away from the input of others, has led to great art, philosophy, and technological advances. And yet, our work culture doesn't allow people the time for it.

When we talk about leisure, we're not just talking about killing time. All downtime is not leisure, because all downtime is not restorative. Doomscrolling is not leisure. The difficulty for us in regaining this sense of real leisure is because the root of it often lies outside the range of what we can do on our own. A break from

87 Daniel A. Gross, "This Is Your Brain on Silence," *Nautilus*, July 31, 2024, getpocket.com/explore/item/this-is-your-brain-on-silence.

work, maybe an hour for lunch, is still a pretty regular part of your everyday schedule. The breaks are there for the sake of work, and they're intended to give you strength for more work. Your lunch hour is not intended to restore your spirit; it's so that you have time to eat a sandwich so you won't pass out on the assembly line.

By contrast, leisure is meant to help you be present in the world around you, to uplift your spirit, and to step beyond the working world to something more. It's more than a break, it's a condition of the soul. Wolfing down a sandwich at your desk while you answer emails is not accomplishing all of that. True leisure can't just be in the service of work, or it becomes part of a useless spiral where we organize our entire lives around work.

Zewna Hitz, an author and professor at St. John's College writes that organizing your entire existence around work is like buying ice cream, immediately selling it for cash, only to use the cash to buy more ice cream.[88] Burnout is so insidious because it can't be solved just by being away from work for a bit. Roger Scruton, a British philosopher, writes in his introduction to Leisure: *The Basis of Culture*, "Leisure is not the cessation of work, but work of another kind, work restored to its human meaning."[89] We've internalized an idea that we don't work to live, but live to work, and it's constantly reinforced by our culture.

When we take a real vacation, when we're really at leisure, we're away from our usual schedules and experiencing life as it unfolds. Looking at a cool ant for as long as we feel like. Our time feels abundant—what's the rush? In fact, time seems to slow down when we're on vacation. This is something called the Holiday Paradox, and it's because vacations tend to mean a lot of new, novel experiences, especially in things that are very different from our usual daily routine.

88 Zena Hitz, "What Is Time For?", *Plough*, August 16, 2023, plough.com/en/topics/life/work/what-is-time-for.

89 Pieper, *Leisure*.

I'm not generally riding go-karts on a Wednesday afternoon, but vacation Caroline is different. She takes long lunches and visits weird museums and never looks at her watch. Her email goes unchecked.

Our lives have a rhythm—coffee, work, lunch, bedtime. Even our nights out tend to revolve around the same activities, the same restaurants, the same movie theaters. On vacation, the stimulation of new sights, foods, and experiences are novel ones, and it actually warps our perception of time. Time seems to slow down to allow us to process all of this new information. Vacations aren't the only thing that have this effect; Claudia Hammond, psychology writer, explains in her book *Time Warped* that time also slows down when we fear for our lives.[90] Things that are of life or death consequences also offer lots of novel information to process, and time does seem to move in slow motion. (Personally, I'd rather go to the beach.)

Leisure is important for our mental health, our sense of self, and yes, for our productivity, creativity, and innovation. We are better people and better workers when we have time to ourselves, away from work. No one is productive every second of their day, no matter what kind of work they do. But it feels like our options to succeed in this work culture are either optimizing our every second, or working an absolute ton of hours. Hustle culture tells us that both of these are excellent options. Capitalism keeps demanding more of us, more of our time, our lives, and we simply have no more to give.

But what is the point of writing all this, what is the point of knowing it, if that is how companies choose to operate? There is a common refrain from those who spend sometimes years of their lives seeking a medical diagnosis, that there is comfort in giving a name to your suffering. Ultimately, it may not matter that you know the name of the thing that's causing you harm and grief. It will continue to cause you harm and grief. Knowing that I have rheumatoid arthritis doesn't make my bones hurt any less. But there is comfort in knowing

90 Maria Popova, "Why Time Slows Down When We're Afraid, Speeds Up as We Age, and Gets Warped on Vacation," *The Marginalian*, n.d., themarginalian.org/2013/07/15/time-warped-claudia-hammond/.

that I am not the only one dealing with it, that there are outside forces making my life harder. Knowing that you aren't the only one uniquely suffering can help you to stop feeling bad for not measuring up, because you have been forced to live in a system that isn't sustainable. Our culture works hard to instill in people the idea that if you aren't being your most productive, you aren't a good person. That same culture is the thing that's making your life harder, and setting unsustainable standards for you.

All of this hustling makes us feel like we don't have the time to do what's essential in our lives. We balance our time, our energy, our work, and our responsibilities, and we find ourselves coming up short. But perhaps we would have more time in our lives *by* doing those essential things. When you fill a jar with small rocks and sand first, there's no more room for the big rocks. We should put the large rocks of those essential things into the jar first, and fill in the other things around them. We assume that everything we do costs us time. But that doesn't really account for the things that energize us, that give us clarity, that allow us peace and relaxation. These are things that actually give us our time back.

If I take a walk out in nature, it takes an hour out of my day, an hour that I could have been working. But I come back from that restored, energized, peaceful. I'm more effective when I return to my work. Writer Mandy Brown wrote in her blog, *Everything Changes,* that when we do what feels essential to us—art, writing, hiking, spending real quality time with people—we are restored. We find our flow, and we make better use of the time we have. So the question is not "How do I make time for this?" We're tried all the life hacks. Instead, in a post titled *Energy Makes Time,* Brown poses a better question—"How does doing what I need make time for everything else?"[91] How will valuing these essential parts of us make our work and our lives better?

91 Mandy Brown, "Energy Takes Time," *Everything Changes,* August 4, 2023, everythingchanges.us/blog/energy-makes-time/.

We don't really understand leisure and its purpose, and that is part of why we don't value it. Leisure is the counter to every aspect of work. Work is useful, leisure is useless. Work is stressful, leisure is relaxation. Work is . . . well, work, and leisure is effortless.

But what is perhaps most important is that when you are at leisure, you are more than just your social use. We can't counter our burnout with leisure time that is just as hurried and stressful as our workday. Leisure is puttering. The time that we spend not just physically, but mentally away from work was once separated and protected, often legally. Sunday was an almost universally shared day off, and thanks to labor organizers, Saturday is recognized as a traditional day off too.

After labor unions won our weekends, people sought out entertainment on those days, which ironically meant that someone had to be working. The need for public services increased, and a desire for these services eventually became an expectation of them. Today, around 30% of full-time workers have weekend shifts according to the US Bureau of Labor Statistics.

There are no holidays where you can't get a burger at a drive-thru. I worked on Christmas Day at a call center to help people fix problems with their newly acquired iPhones. That couldn't have waited one day? Fast food restaurants might close early for Thanksgiving, but they aren't going to close all day. When that time isn't legally protected, only people with leverage are able to refuse work then.

But even when we are technically "off" these days, it's not like we're unreachable. We don't have any time that's ours that is truly protected, it's always at least a bit in danger of being infringed upon by work. It means that our leisure time doesn't feel abundant, it doesn't feel truly free. Leisure is something that we must cultivate, to recognize as worthwhile and seek out, and to protect. France introduced a law in 2017 called "the right to disconnect," which legally protects workers' right to ignore work emails outside of work hours. They're legally protecting their time.

This lack of protected time away from work can make it harder for us to gather. Robert Putnam, political scientist, wrote a followup to his book, *Bowling Alone*, in 2015 and found that our social networks are now made of fewer people, and less non-family ties, than they used to be. We've become more suspicious of each other, more afraid of lawsuits and retaliation. Community is built by developing trust and meaning together, and when we don't spend time together to do that, we focus inward instead. Communities meet online instead of in physical spaces, and third spaces where people could just hang out have started to disappear.

Spaces that do still exist are often less central, and less welcoming to loiterers than they used to be. You can't sit together in a coffee shop if you aren't buying anything. Malls are requiring parental supervision for anyone under eighteen. Many public spaces that don't charge for entry still charge for parking, or because of liability, they aren't open when they aren't staffed. The places where we used to form informal ties are harder to come by.

There are few truly free spaces where people can gather. We need the time and the space to relate to each other as people, to slow down enough to make meaningful connections. The way that our lives are scheduled around work makes these kinds of deep friendships hard to make, but also hard to maintain. Connections like these require time, and many industries have variable schedules.

If you have different days off from one week to the next, and you don't get your schedule much in advance, it feels hard to commit to plans. As an Australian friend of mine once said, "One day's notice for an event? Buddy, I work in hospo." We are encouraged toward a life of efficiency, that doesn't make room for connection. Hanging out with friends isn't efficient.

But what can we do? We can't put the toothpaste back into the tube, and we have become accustomed to services being 24/7. We can fight for changes that make it easier to gather, to keep space for them both mentally and physically. We can push for scheduling that's more consistent, that perhaps isn't optimized by an algorithm to produce the leanest possible shift, but by a human person that allows workers to schedule their lives more than a week in advance.

Social groups can themselves keep a consistent schedule, which offers a break from planning and decision fatigue. Groups like the PTA, story time, quilt guilds—all of these organizations use reliability to make it easier for people to be involved. They meet at the same time, same day, same place, every week. I joined a community orchestra that meets every Tuesday at 7pm. I can't imagine sending out an email chain every week to get an orchestra's worth of people to otherwise agree on a time and space. The reliability means that we can all build our schedules around it. We can also mentally commit to the idea that leisure is a necessary part of our existence, and that committing to overwork instead means that all of those extra hours are pushing essential experiences out of our lives. Something has to give, and for once, it should be work.

Leisure allows for connection. It gives us the time to pursue art and hobbies, the time to putter and explore, the time to be with other people. It gives us the time to be with ourselves, to withdraw from input for a while, and have the kind of solitude that leads to deep thought and great accomplishments.

When you understand what leisure gives you, it's easy to see the value of it, to see why we need to protect it. The kind of solidarity that we need to build to make real change starts with us spending quality time together, and that requires leisure time. It allows us to see all the things that we have in common.

Our lives belong to us, and we can do what we want with them. Being together reminds us of that. The alternative is just the endless grind of work, a net for catching our days. There is more to our lives than optimizing them for the most amount of work that we can do. But how do we combat an entire culture?

Four-Day Workweek

Setting healthy boundaries, creating a slower paced routine, and self-care are all things that we can do on our own. But we also need big, systemic changes to create a better work-life balance for everyone. There are policies that we can fight for, and work toward, that will improve our relationship to our work. That will help us to stave off burnout, and push back against the creeping demands of overwork.

One of those policies is fighting a concept that feels like an immutable truth—that a workweek should be eight hours a day, five days a week. A weekend simply is, and will always be, two days. But why?

One hundred years ago, Henry Ford decided that a five-day, forty-hour workweek was the optimal schedule, and the consensus was that he was nuts. It would never work, and no reasonable manufacturers would ever adopt the change. They all had many of the same concerns that modern companies have now about the idea of a four-day workweek. Primarily, that there is already too much work to be done without taking an entire workday away. If I'm overworked now, how much worse would it be with eight less hours every week? And employees still expect to be paid for those eight hours? They haven't earned it! Ford's contemporaries said the exact same thing. The standard then, working an average of sixty hours over six days each week, likely seemed as much a core truth to them as our weekly schedule does to us now. It was considered normal, even necessary. How did Ford ever sell the auto industry on such a drastic change?

He discovered that more work didn't necessarily mean better work. In fact, long hours and longer weeks resulted in costly mistakes by overtired employees, and employee turnover due to the working conditions meant spending money on training new hires. In 1914, long before Roosevelt signed a labor law package that included maximum hours and instituted overtime pay, Ford realized that having to train replacements for the employees who quit was costing him a lot of money.

Employee turnover is very expensive. Every new employee has a break-in period, where they're still learning and not as productive as they will one day be. Every existing employee who walked off the line to find a better job slowed down production until they could be replaced. To incentivize those workers to stay, Ford doubled their salary. To reduce expensive mistakes by overtired employees, he cut their hours. More pay and shorter hours for his workers directly led to more cash in Ford's pockets.

He argued that it would put more money in the pockets of other companies as well. Having an extra day off would encourage his workers to take vacations, to shop for more clothes for their leisure time, to eat at restaurants, and to need more transportation in vehicles (did you know that he sold vehicles?) In short, his workers would spend more money—it was a service to the economy.

Ford proved that workers were both more productive and more dedicated to a company that wasn't grinding them into a fine powder. He showed other businesses that workers could accomplish just as much in five days as they could in six. Of course, Ford didn't change the landscape of our workweek all on his own. Having a high profile businessman adopt the change helped, but labor movements protested, struck, and lobbied for shorter workdays. One of the first demands of the organized labor movement was reducing the ten hour workday. By the nineteenth century, they'd cut the average workweek down to sixty hours, before Ford encouraged the change to forty.

Nobody made him do this, there wasn't a law at the time, and other manufacturers weren't leading the charge. But he saw the benefit, and changed the way that he scheduled and compensated his employees. If you're in a position to make these kinds of decisions in your own business, you don't have to wait for laws to change either. You can look at the data, and do what's best for your business. Which, it turns out in the long run, looks a lot like what's best for your employees.

There's no natural law that says how many hours we should all work each week, there is simply a standard that we all agree to.

Historically, companies push for more of our time, and we push back. But eventually, people like Henry Ford began to study how they could increase worker productivity, and they realized that overwork had some serious downsides.

Perhaps it's time to take another look at what the optimal workweek is. We do not have to work forty-hour weeks simply because we've been working forty-hour weeks, or simply because other people do. It's our standard now, but in the whole of humans' working history, it hasn't been the standard all that long. All of it seems inevitable, in retrospect. Of course people would protest working day and night, and of course working one hundred hours a week makes for an exhausted and ineffective employee. Obviously we should have two days for weekends, which is objectively the correct amount of time to be away from our jobs.

But none of it was inevitable. It took vision and work to make these drastic changes. It took activists pushing for changes to be made. It took people with power instituting those changes. It will take those same things to change our work standards again. Modern work requires a change in our mindset about work. With more careers being potentially automated, done by robots or AI, or simply done by far fewer people than it required in the past, it's time to move past the idea of what people have earned, and to reconsider what they deserve. For our work-obsessed culture, that's a big ask.

Our current workweek was optimized to get the best work out of men on an automotive assembly line, and going home to wives who didn't work outside of their homes. This wasn't every person's reality, but that's the demographic this was standardized for.

Our work, and our lifestyle, has changed enormously since the 1930s. The work that we're doing, and the way that we do it, is different now. Even people who still work in the automotive industry are doing it differently than we did one hundred years ago. Computers have made us more efficient and productive, measurably so. In an hour, a modern office worker can do what would have taken them five hours to do in 1970, according to a 2017 article in *The Conversation* by Joshua Krook.[92] We could complete a full 1970s workday in about an hour and a half today. In his essay *Economic Possibilities for Our Grandchildren*, economist and philosopher John Maynard Keynes famously predicted that we'd have a fifteen-hour workweek by 2030, thanks to these consistent improvements to our efficiency. To his credit, there is still time. Yet as of today, even though we do more work in less time than we ever have, our wages aren't keeping pace with the sheer amount of work we're completing, and our hours haven't decreased. Instead, we're filling all that time with more work.

Data on our stagnant wages, and the benefits to cutting work hours, have existed for some time now. But the idea of a four-day workweek is still plagued by many of the questions asked of Ford by his contemporaries.

To start, aren't we just shoving more work into less hours? Some employees have expressed concern that their work would just become more intense and stressful as they're fitting the same tasks into even less time. But companies who are thriving on a reduced schedule worked smarter, not harder. They looked critically at their operations, and found ways to work more efficiently without working more.

Many years ago, I worked for a company that made sports jerseys, and I was in the digital cutting department. I had two jobs there, essentially. One job was picking, not unlike Amazon warehouse workers, but with significantly less possible options to pick from. When an order came in for a Crosby jersey, I would run around our stacks to pull the 8s and 7s that needed to be sent off to ironing and embroidery. If I reached for a piece and found the bin was empty, I did my other job, which was to make more of them. This job had a very easily quantified output—how many orders did I pick? How many new files did I set up and cut? It's not the type of work where you're making progress toward an outcome over days, or weeks, or months.

92 Joshua Krook, "Whatever Happened to the Fifteen-Hour Workweek?", *The Conversation*, October 8, 2017, theconversation.com/whatever-happened-to-the-15-hour-workweek-84781.

An order was either finished or it wasn't. It truly didn't make sense to measure my productivity by how many hours I spent in the building doing those things. And yet, most work is gauged exactly that way.

I found, a few months into working there, that I completed three times as many orders during my shift, alone, as the multiple people working second shift did combined. Likely because they'd been there awhile, and knew better. Because even though I met and then exceeded the goals they'd set for my day, I still had to work the same mandatory overtime as everyone else. For working super efficiently, I was rewarded with more work. Not with more money, better benefits, or less hours. Just fill more orders, because you're here for another 6 hours, and what else are you gonna do? When faced with that situation, most of us spread our work out.

If the company's original goal is to fill fifty orders in a day, and they find that I can do that in four hours, they're not going to simply let me work a four-hour day. Their thinking is that if I can fill those fifty orders in the first half of my day, then I could surely do one hundred in an eight-hour day, and they'll make more money. But people are not machines, and the more likely outcome is that their employees will end up spreading the same amount of work across more hours, and you're getting those same fifty orders completed. You can't ask people to sprint for the length of a marathon; humans aren't built for it. And you aren't really giving them any incentive to. Why would an employee work faster and harder, knowing they still have another ten hours of mandatory overtime that week no matter how much they get done?

Just because your employees are physically at work for eight hours doesn't mean that it takes eight hours to get their work done. A huge point of contention for companies when it comes to cutting hours is the idea that employees are doing less work without decreasing their pay. But it's a shift in paying people for their actual output, instead of simply paying them for their time.

If you can produce fifty widgets in four hours instead of eight, why aren't you still paid for producing fifty widgets? Why should you be paid less just because your job took you less time? We're subject to the Effort Trap. As Dmytro Okunyv, founder of Zurich-based software company Chanty, shared with *Digiday*, "It's no longer interesting for a company when staff is working, only what they produce when they are."[93] Why should I care if you finished your work in two hours or six, if the work is done? For service industries with set hours, this can certainly be more complicated, but it's not impossible. Buffer, a social media management website, uses a staggered schedule, so that they have customer service coverage 24/7 despite working a shorter week. What we see in four-day workweek trials is that a lot of the hours we all spend in the office, or otherwise on the clock, go to waste. In one survey by Zapier, nearly a third of people said that they only spend four to five hours every day doing their core work function. Most spent less than three hours per day on creative work, and less than three hours per week on strategic work.[94] What is sucking up the rest of their time?

Largely, something that Ryan Brewslow of Bolt calls "theater work" in a Twitter post. It's work that's designed to look good, versus work that actually addresses your core function as a company. Companies that look to reduce their hours often become more efficient through dropping this theater work, and of those who have participated in a major four-day workweek trial, 78% of the employees didn't feel like their workload increased, despite the reduction in hours according to a pilot study by Autonomy and 4 Day Week Global.[95] They aren't shoving the same amount of tasks into less hours, but are looking more critically at which tasks are truly important. Brewslow

93 Tony Case, "Coronavirus Pandemic Has More Employers Experimenting with Four-Day Workweek," *Digiday*, February 1, 2021, digiday.com/media/four-day-work-week/.

94 Zapier Editorial Team, "Meetings Aren't Killing Productivity; Data Entry Is," *Zapier*, July 23, 2021, zapier.com/blog/report-how-office-workers-spend-time/.

95 "The Results Are In: The UK's Four-Day Workweek Pilot," Autonomy.com, February 2023, autonomy.work/portfolio/uk4dwpilotresults/.

shared on his Twitter account that he believes two days of mindful, conscious work are better for the company than five days of going through the motions.[96]

We waste a lot of our time doing work that is not important, that doesn't serve our core functions. Meetings are a common place to find this theater work happening, and I have often said that they're where work goes to die. Many organizations trying out a reduced workweek have made their meetings shorter, less frequent, and with a clearer agenda. So many time-wasting processes can be cut out by asking questions, like "Is this necessary?" and "Who is it necessary for?" You don't have to include every employee in a meeting simply because they're in the office that day. When you really sit and take the time to look at a workday, the parts that simply don't need to be there become clear.

Some employees may worry that this will lead to the discovery that the work they're doing is unnecessary. But as we all keep saying, there is more than enough work that needs to be done. Dropping processes that don't serve us doesn't lead to mass layoffs, but to freeing up time for those workers to do something more important. When I started a new position as a webmaster for a hospital, I was getting several emails a day from the nursing staff asking me to turn their Word files into PDFs. It was time that I could better spend elsewhere, and an unnecessary step that slowed down the workflow for the nurses, so I took the time to show them how to do it themselves. Fixing that inefficiency didn't lead the company to cut my position, it just meant that I had more time to focus on the work that I actually needed to do.

So a four-day workweek doesn't mean losing important work time, or losing one-fifth of every worker's productivity. Yet one of the biggest concerns voiced about reducing work hours is that people are being paid for something that they did not earn. But the truth is,

96 Ryan Breslow, Twitter Post, January 4, 2020, 10:08 AM, twitter.com/ryan-breslow/status/1478564004356317186; Giulia Carbonaro, "Every U.S. Company With a 4-Day Workweek—Full List," *Newsweek*, April 20, 2022, newsweek.com%2Fevery-us-company-4-day-workweek-full-list-1697943.

they have earned it, and have been over-earning it for decades. We produce more, we accomplish more, and yet wages don't reflect our increased productivity.

People have moved toward squaring this fact through "quiet quitting," which was not quitting at all, but deciding to stop putting in hours of extra time that was going unpaid. How else can an individual bring their wages in line with their productivity? How do you level that playing field? Reducing hours can make the math work. These people aren't getting something they haven't earned; they're accomplishing the same things in less time now, and shouldn't be penalized for it. Why should they be paid less for being efficient?

Some companies have used a four-day work week to attract employees post-Covid (inasmuch as we are, actually, post-Covid). While companies were recovering, they weren't able to attract talented staff with pay increases and offered a shorter workweek instead. This offers a competitive advantage for both recruitment and employee retention. Something to view as another benefit, like vacation time or home office stipends. In 4 Day Week Global's UK pilot program, 15% of employees said that you could not pay them enough to go back to a five day week, and half of them said they would only consider it for at least a 25% raise.[97] Our time is valuable to us, and these numbers should be of great interest to companies who are trying to recruit top talent.

But does this really work? Are companies seriously thriving while they pay their employees the same amount for 416 less work hours every year? The data says yes. 4 Day Week Global is not the first ever four-day workweek trial, but it's the biggest one so far, and they found out just about exactly what you'd expect. When asked if they were going to continue with their reduced hours, 92% of the companies in the trial said yes.[98] Managers and staff said that the trial

97 "The Results Are In," autonomy.work/portfolio/uk4dwpilotresults/.

98 Ibid

really made them think about how their workplace ran, to rethink what they did and how they did it.

It's difficult to carve out the time to do this kind of thoughtful assessment of your workplace, on top of the regular work that you're already doing, but most companies found it to be a hugely worthwhile use of their time. Researchers wondered what made companies opt to do all this work, to participate in the trial, when they could just as easily continue to work the way they always had. Some companies did see it as a way to maximize their competitive advantages and attract talent. Others spoke of protecting their human capital, which is a gross phrase, but did motivate those in charge to look out for the well-being of their employees. The pandemic gave these managers a new insight into their staff's personal lives that they hadn't had before Zoom meetings became the norm. They watched us suffer through mental health difficulties and bereavements. They met our pets and our kids. Senior management felt that it increased their sense of moral responsibility to their employees, and made them more sensitive to the business need for a healthy workforce.[99] It's pretty bonkers that senior management was unable to feel this empathy toward their employees without seeing them bleary-eyed in their 120-square foot apartment during weekly standups, but we'll take what solidarity we can get.

Truly, anyone who has enjoyed a three-day weekend at any point in their lives will not be surprised by all the benefits from working shorter hours. We'll be printing up "people enjoy working less" in the next issue of *Obvious Research Quarterly*. Still, the 4 Day Global study took this seriously, and gave formal before and after surveys to gauge employees' feelings about their reduced hours and well-being. Employees reported less stress, less burnout, less fatigue. Their mental and physical health improved. Their work-life balance was better. Food tasted better, probably (that one wasn't included in the survey, actually.)

99 Ibid

Time is a finite resource, and modern humans are stretched very, very thin. Having just one more day every week that is ours to do what we want feels downright miraculous. Fifty-two extra days a year is incredibly precious to all of us, but some fields benefit very specifically from having distance from their work, like those with emotionally demanding jobs. Organizations that support patients with brain injuries, teach special education, or advise families in the foster system really need that time away from the emotional pressures of their work.

Other companies are dealing with industry-wide problems of overwork that can be common in creative and tech fields. Video game studios, for example, pointed to endless cases of crunch and burnout. One studio that participated in the trial said that they hoped to be different from other companies in their industry, where people are often treated like "economic units." Their CEO said that long hours weren't helping their workers, and they weren't helping the studio either. If you know that you're stuck at the office until 10 pm, what's the hurry to get your work done?[100]

This concern for doing right by their employees, and giving them the downtime they need to do their best work, was one that was frequently brought up as the reason for signing on for the trial. Cutting a day of work means that employees are better rested and thus better at their jobs, with more time to rejuvenate their spirits.

I have worked a four-day workweek at a design studio, and also at a mid-sized regional hospital as part of my FMLA. It's a remarkable difference. I had no issues completing my work, communication with others at the office wasn't a problem, and I had an extra day a week to rest and run errands. I didn't find myself having to tend to work during my off hours to get things done, or stressing out over trying to fit everything into four days. I had a midweek day off at both places, rather than the more typical three-day weekend, and still found that I

100 Ibid

felt considerably less stress and fatigue than I had at any of my forty hour per week jobs.

Running errands is the primary thing employees are fitting in during their extra day off. What the study called "life admin" were tasks that bleed into the workday, because handling some of those things during work hours is the only way that many of us can get any free time. Things like calling to make doctor's appointments, grocery shopping, even chores around the house. Shorter work hours align better with the way that modern people work. As more of us are dual income households, we find ourselves jamming errands and household chores into our weekends, which no longer feel relaxing or restorative. For those of us with kids, our weekends are often filled with their activities as well, and having the extra time to do our life admin is invaluable. Childcare, however, is a bit easier to put a hard number to. Having to pay for one less day of childcare per week would save us, in the state of Pennsylvania, $1,820 annually, which is on par with the national average. But in some states, like Massachusetts, those savings reach almost $5,000.

It's unsurprising that people are happier and healthier when they spend less of their time working. It doesn't take a major global study to figure that out. But if you're trying to convince your workplace to try out a four-day week, or you're in a position to decide this for your own company, you'll also need to consider whether it's a sustainable practice for business. The answer is, again, an absolutely resounding yes. Companies that participated in 4 Day Week Global's study thrived. Their revenue increased 35% over previous years. Employee turnover dropped 57%, and their employee numbers stayed steady throughout the trial, which was conducted during a time when workers were quitting their jobs at record rates. They made more money while working less, they were better able to retain staff, and their employees even missed less work. Employees were not only happier with their lives outside of work, but they were more satisfied with their jobs. Happier people are more engaged employees, and most workers said that they were doing a better job now that they were working less hours.

The success of work-from-home policies has been a catalyst for companies to reconsider more things about the way they work. If we can work from anywhere, what else can we do? Why not be innovative in other areas, with other policies? Or as Art Schectman, President of Elephant Ventures put it in my phone interview with him in 2023, "Why change one thing when we can change everything?"[101]

Well-rested and happy employees are more engaged, more creative, and more innovative. Ryan Brewslow published a Twitter thread on Bolt's change to a four-day week, and said that most workers today are exhausted. That fatigue kills creativity and innovation. Bolt finds that the problem with remote work isn't people working less, but people working far too much. When you're overtired, your standards go down, but even more dangerously, you start to always look for the path of least resistance. A five-day workweek barely allows enough time to take care of necessities, but an extra day off gives you time to actually rest and to develop your interests. These experiences and perspectives fuel new ideas. Brewslow said that if a four-day week only made people happier with no other benefits, that alone would be worth it.[102] But this study finds that there are significant benefits to employees and companies alike.

With all of this research and data showing that staring at computer screens for forty hours a week is counterproductive, why is it so hard to get more companies on board with a change in our work hours? One major issue is that our culture struggles with the concept of "enough." There could always be more—more work, more money, we can be more and do more and have more. This is not a screed against ambition, it's important to have goals in your life and work to

---

101 Art Shectman (president of Elephant Ventures), interview by Caroline Moore, June 2023.

102 Breslow, twitter.com/ryanbreslow/status/1478564004356317186.

strive for. But it's also important to recognize when it's enough, when you're getting diminishing returns for all your effort. It's hard for us to recognize when we hit that point.

In a business, there's always something that can be done, and something that can be a billable hour. Consider that your business is to clean your house. You've done everything that really needs to be done, and it's taken you four hours. It's clean, it looks lovely, it's up to your standard of living. But you've got eight hours to fill today. Could you find something more to do? Sure. You could find some useful things to do, maybe scrubbing the baseboards or washing all the windows. If you're still desperate to fill time, you can find some less useful things to do, like dusting the furnace or alphabetizing the soup cans.

The point is, that you can surely find something to do to fill your time, but is it something that needs to be done today? This week? At all? Is it essential to your core service? How much of what you do at your real, actual paid job is busywork to fill time? It's easy to say that we couldn't reduce our work hours, because look at how busy we already are! It's hard to say when it's enough, we've done enough.

The easiest thing is often to follow the momentum of what we're already doing. To carry on as though Henry Ford had brought down our one true workweek from a mountain on stone tablets. It takes far more time and effort to really consider what would be best for our business and for our employees, but it is worth it.

Consider the benefits of putting more thought into what the optimal amount of time is to spend at work now, today, given the kind of work that we're doing. What we do, and how we do it? Study after study shows that happy workers, those whose work aligns with their lives and values, are simply more productive workers. When we're treated like cogs, not people, it's harder for us to do our jobs. In Charles Duhigg's book, *The Power of Habit,* he describes a study done by psychology professor Mark Muraven, where he asked two groups of people to ignore a plate of cookies in front of them. In the first group, he told everyone the purpose of the experiment, and thanked them for their time. In the second group, he simply said, "Don't eat those." The first group had better results.[103]

When people have a sense of control over their experience, when they feel that it's done as a choice or something that helps someone else, the task that's being asked of them feels less arduous. But when they feel like they're just following orders, with no real autonomy in the situation, that task feels harder to do, and they're less motivated to bother. It's better for both employees and employers when workers have control over their lives, but making that change boils down to our culture's ability to change its views and its values.

We keep glorifying overwork and burning out our employees even in the face of research that overwhelmingly shows that a reduction in work hours is better for everyone, research that has existed for some time. We need a few big companies willing to lead the way, as Henry Ford once did. Everyone thought that Ford was crazy at first, but later those same manufacturers were copying his success. Many companies involved in the 4 Day Week Global trial liked the idea of making history. Leading the charge against what they see as an outdated model. Nick Bands, managing director of Unilever in New Zealand says, "We believe the old ways of working are outdated and no longer fit for purpose" in an article for World Economic Forum. Their goal now is to measure performance on output, not time.[104] "Technology allows us to work faster than ever, and I truly believe a 40-hour workweek is outdated," says Aaron Metzger, founder of Genius Digital Marketing in Colleyville, Texas in Success Magazine.[105]

---

103 Charles Duhigg, *The Power of Habit: Why We Do What We Do in Life and Business* (Random House Trade Paperbacks, 2014).

104 Kayleigh Bateman, "New Study Shows Four-Day Working Week to Be a Success," World Economic Forum, January 31, 2022, weforum.org/agenda/2022/01/four-day-week-work-life-balance-trial/.

105 Alex Frost, "The Four-Day Workweek Massive Pilot Results Are in—It Was a 'Resounding Success,' " *Success*, September 19, 2024, success.com/four-day-workweek-study/.

A big shift feels more possible now, thanks in part to a huge change in work patterns and attitudes following the Covid pandemic. We became accustomed to more flexible working schedules, to remote work, and to the better work-life balance that came with those changes. We saw what was possible, and many of us don't want to go back to the way we used to structure our work. We have shown that we can make drastic changes, and find success in them, but we will still have to fight against the same arguments that were made against adding Saturday to the weekend way back in the 1930s.

Companies and individuals alike get hung up on the idea that people would be working less and yet earn just as much money, which is exactly what happened when we moved to a five-day standard week decades ago. These trials show the same thing that manufacturers discovered then, that people aren't doing less work, they're simply doing it in less hours, and generally making less mistakes. The companies that have taken part in these trials still delivered on all their objectives. These kinds of pilots have shown success all over, and research has been overwhelmingly positive. All we need now is for companies to have the vision to lead the way.

Organizations looking for inspiration to change don't need to look far. They now have access to an ever growing base of companies who have implemented a shorter schedule, who can offer their insight. Kickstarter, Headspace, Uplift, Buffer, and Basecamp have all offered four-day weeks. A customer support agent at Buffer has called the change "a godsend" according to Business Insider[106] Awin, a Berlin based company with one thousand workers across the globe, working across time zones, has adopted a four-day week permanently. Time Magazine reported that the benefits are very clear: employees are

---

106 Katie Canales, "Corporate America Is Starting to Embrace the Four-Day Workweek," *Business Insider*, June 26, 2021, businessinsider.com/four-day-work-week-companies-adopting-longer-weekends-2021-6.

happier and healthier, companies are more productive and efficient, and more able to recruit and retain staff.[107]

Michael Leiter, an independent organizational psychologist and consultant, sees it often in health care, where he does most of his work. He says in Scientific American that stress in the workplace is making it harder to hold on to talented people, and to recruit new hires.[108] People are demanding more changes in how their work is organized. Companies who are willing to make the change find it's a huge benefit to recruiting talent.

Once, companies said that remote work was simply impossible, a business could not run that way. Disabled folks fought for years to be able to do their jobs remotely, only to be told it could not be done. Then Covid happened, and wouldn't you know it, remote work is very much possible. The pandemic changed the way we look at our lives and our work, and the idea of what's possible. This was an enormous, drastic change to the way we've been working for most of our lives, and we just . . . did it. With very little planning, or training, we dove into a whole different way of working. We've proved that even huge companies that are filled with red tape are able to make big changes.

Being forced to work at home at the beginning of 2020 gave a lot of people more time away from work than they'd ever had before. Long commutes were over, and we were home for our lunches and breaks. We used the time to do laundry, take a walk, or spend time with our kids and spouses. When companies wanted to return to business as usual, we didn't want to give that time back. We have greater expectations for flexible or hybrid working now.

---

107 Lisa Abend, "Why 2023 Could Finally Be the Year of the Four-Day Workweek," *Time Magazine*, January 19, 2023, time.com/6248369/4-day-workweek-2023/.

108 Jan Dönges and Sophie Bushwick, "A Four-Day Workweek Reduces Stress without Hurting Productivity," *Scientific American*, March 7, 2023, scientificamerican.com/article/a-four-day-workweek-reduces-stress-without-hurting-productivity/.

And companies have found it to be a competitive advantage—they could hire talent from anywhere, no commute required. Smart companies, who want to remain competitive, have rolled remote or hybrid work into their policies. They've embraced flexible scheduling. Many managers were somehow surprised to find that people working from home were actually working, and that led to more trust in their employees than they'd had before. When employees feel valued, when they're allowed to choose how, when, or where to work, they do their best work.

The pandemic upended everything about our work lives and allowed big changes to our regular routines. We made a huge change to the way that we work, with nearly no advance planning. Changing the structure of our workweek, changing our mindset from one that values only hours logged to one that values what's actually being produced, may seem too big a change to make. Taking the time to re-optimize for the kind of work we're doing now, to give our brains the space and downtime that they need to do innovative, creative work may seem like a pipe dream. But so did working from your living room, once.

We have seen what kind of large scale change is possible—look at what your own workplace has already done! You may be surprised by just how drastic a change you are capable of making. Given all the research that shows improved financial health, employee retention, and engagement among their workers, the four-day workweek is certainly a change worth making.

CEO Pay Ratios

Simply spending less of our time working is one way to improve our relationship with work, but there are other aspects of building a company that can have a huge impact on worker morale, autonomy, and work-life balance—all things that ultimately affect our propensity for burnout. One such factor, that can either worsen or help ameliorate income inequality, is the CEO pay ratio. It's worth examining why those ratios are often so high, and what we as workers can do about it.

This pay ratio is the difference between the highest paid employee (usually, but not always, the CEO) and the average employee's salary. If you asked a random person on the street, they would likely report that these gaps in pay are large, but most of us underestimate just how huge the gaps can be. In 1965, Gawker reports, the CEO to average worker ratio was around 20 to 1.[109] So if the average worker made $30,000 a year, the CEO would be making $600,000 a year. Today, that ratio has risen to 260 to 1, according to the BBC, which means that if an average worker makes the same $30,000 a year, the CEO would now make $7.8 million annually. It's a big jump. CEO pay rose nearly 900% between 1978 and 2012, but have CEOs gotten 900% better at their jobs?[110] Who is in charge of deciding how much CEOs get paid?

Compensation committees make these decisions, and the compensation packages (which generally include more than just a salary) are self-perpetuating. Committees benchmark these salaries, and no committee is going to say that their company isn't above average. The Atlantic explains that CEOs will get benchmarked at the 75th, or even 90th percentile, because that's how the committee views the company, as better than most. They set the compensation at $20 million, and that becomes the standard for a CEO in that percentile. When their peers are later benchmarked by their own committees, their pay goes up too.[111] Every time a CEO gets a high benchmark and a pay bump, they're setting a higher baseline for the next committee.

---

109 Hamilton Nolan, "What's an Acceptable Ratio of CEO Pay to Worker Pay?", *Gawker*, September 18, 2013, gawkerarchives.com/whats-an-acceptable-ratio-of-ceo-pay-to-worker-pay-1342761039

110 Christine Ro, "The Push to Penalize Big Corporations with Huge Pay Gaps," *BBC*, June 14, 2021, bbc.com/worklife/article/20210610-the-push-to-penalise-big-corporations-with-huge-pay-gaps.

111 Steven Clifford, "How Companies Actually Decide What to Pay CEOs," *The Atlantic*, June 14, 2017, theatlantic.com/business/archive/2017/06/how-companies-decide-ceo-pay/530127/.

CEOs aren't the only ones raking in huge piles of cash, of course. Movie stars and famous athletes are also making millions, but there's a lot less ire directed their way for it. Possibly because we're seeing what value they add to our lives in a more direct way. We see Ryan Reynolds on the big screen, or we watch Cristiano Ronaldo winning soccer matches. Who knows what the CEO at Unilever is doing all day long.

The employees at any given company are the ones who actually produce the goods or perform a service—those are the people you actually see. So when their CEO makes 260 times more than they do, it seems unfair in a way that Stephen King making bank for the books he writes doesn't. More than that, people are less directly harmed by Lebron James's paycheck. Your ticket cost doesn't change based on his salary going up or down, but there's a case to be made that huge CEO salaries do harm their employees, the economy on the whole, and even their own company.

Big gaps in pay like these drive inequality, and they help to further widen gender and racial disparities in pay, since women and people of color make up a large percentage of low wage workers, but only a tiny share of corporate leaders. Executives chasing bigger bonuses have been blamed in part for the 2008 financial crisis, and current CEO pay practices incentivize reckless behavior that lacks concern for their employees' welfare. It rewards them for cutting jobs, accelerating climate change, and dodging taxes. While companies report record profits, we watch all of that money go straight to the top. Extreme pay disparities also undermine employee morale, and raise turnover rates. It's a problem that causes both social and economic harm. The AFL-CIO, America's largest union, argues in Fast Company magazine that CEO pay is even causing inflation.[112] Admittedly, I'm no economist, but I'm pretty sure that inflation is bad.

112 Clint Rainey, "The Age of 'Greedflation' Is Here: See How Obscene CEO-to-Worker Pay Ratios Are Right Now, *Fast Company*, July 18, 2022, fastcompany.com/90770163/the-age-of-greedflation-is-here-see-how-obscene-ceo-to-worker-pay-ratios-are-right-now/.

But what can we do? Certainly these compensation committees aren't asking my opinion on CEO pay. We could hope for high level executives to have a crisis of conscience about just how much more they receive than the people who make their business possible. One, arguably superior, solution that's been suggested is to tie executives' bonuses to metrics like how employees feel about their working conditions, which would incentivize them to do better by their employees. Behavioral economics research by Alexander Pepper of the London School of Economics suggests that tying a generous salary and bonuses to specific outcomes like these could be more effective than basing them on how the company stock performs.[113] As we're seeing here, what is best for the workers often turns out to be what's best for the company in the long run.

There are also legislative options to pursue. The SEC (Securities and Exchange Commission) has required companies to report their CEO pay ratios, and some have suggested that a maximum ratio should be enforced by law. If executives want to keep their big paychecks, they would have to raise the wages of their employees, too. Some states have imposed higher taxes on companies whose gaps are over a set ratio, and Congress is looking at a bill in 2024 that would make that national.

Of course, enormous corporations are very skilled at weaseling out of laws like this, like a previous 1993 law that was meant to lower executive salaries, but instead led to them giving bonuses instead of set wages. This is often the case when you see founders very publicly making their salary $1. These regulations do, however, at least make them work a little harder to cheat the system. And if we decided it wasn't worth it to make a law, because companies would break them anyway, then what is the point for having any laws for anyone at all? Legislation isn't a perfect solution, but it is a useful pursuit.

113 Alexander Pepper, "The Behavioural Economics of Executive Incentives," *NHRD Network Journal* 14, no. 2 (2020), doi.org/10.1177/26314541209530.

Not everyone thinks that these kinds of laws will be effective, though, and some even insist they would do more harm than good. Kevin Murphy, a professor of economics at the University of Southern California, contends in an article for the BBC that taxing pay ratios would mean a tax on specifically those industries that hire mostly low-lage workers. That it would be unfair to them.

If these companies don't want to pay the tax, they can fix the disparity by paying their CEOs less and their workers more, just like any other industry. But the average worker at Starbucks makes less than the average worker at Goldman Sachs, and thus the CEO of Starbucks would have to take a pay cut to close that gap. They contend that they'll have a harder time attracting talent for CEO positions if they aren't paid more money than any of us will ever see in our lives. (But their companies keep telling me that if I don't take their lowball offer for employment then someone else will, so maybe that'll work out for CEO positions too.)

Steve Pearlstein, who has won a Pulitzer for his financial writing, shared with the Harvard Business School Business Insights blog that he finds it very odd that boards of directors will set high salaries, options, bonuses, and shares in the company for their top executives, yet they don't seem to notice that money might be important to the people who keep a business running.[114] They're not viewing their employees as assets, the way they do their CEOs.

This is one solution, to agitate for legislative changes. To support our representatives when they back laws that aim to bring down the CEO pay ratio, and yell at them when they don't. We can continue to make a fuss about this being a real problem. Some of us are also in positions of power to make changes ourselves. If you're running a business, if you have employees to manage yourself, then you can do better. You can decide how your business is structured, and offer

---

114 Mike Wheeler, "A Bold Wage That Still Pays Off," Harvard Business School Online, January 11, 2018, online.hbs.edu/blog/post/three-years-ago-this-boss-set-a-usd70-000-minimum-wage-for-his-employees-and-the-move-is-still-paying-off/.

a pay scale that's fair. You can set a CEO pay ratio that isn't extreme, and actually allow your profits to trickle down. We may not convince Exxon to do this out of the goodness of their heart, but you have an opportunity to reconsider the way that things are usually done, and decide to do it differently.

There are companies out there who are doing this voluntarily. You can be inspired by them and you can support them. They may not have any legal obligation to create a better workplace, but they feel that they have an ethical one. In 2013, Satoru Iwata cut his pay by 50% to avoid layoffs at Nintendo. Where many companies decide to improve their financial performance by laying off their workers, he didn't. He shared with *Game Developer* that their employees make valuable contributions, and that laying off those employees won't help to strengthen Nintendo's business in the long run. He was looking out for the health of his company in the future, and not chasing short-term gains. When you view your employees as an asset, and not as an expense, you do what you must to retain them.

Similarly, Dan Price, the CEO of Gravity Payments, cut his own salary so that he could give his staff a $70,000 minimum wage, which was a significant bump from their previous average salary of $48,000. He said that the change was about values, and he hopes that like those who have moved to four-day workweeks, he can inspire others to follow his lead. He was called a lunatic and a socialist, and accused of meddling with the free market. His own brother, a 30% shareholder in the company, sued him. But he felt a responsibility to his employees, and a need to run his business more ethically.

Price was very happy to report the human successes, in the way that his employee's lives have improved. One employee was able to rent somewhere much closer than his previous two-hour commute, and had more time for things he enjoyed in life, like playing guitar. Another was able to move out of an apartment that didn't even have running water. In The Guardian online, Price says "The fact I created an environment where this was happening, because of a company I'd designed . . . people were being exploited. People I care about, who've helped me so much, now have more dignity. The distraction of not having enough to cover the basics has gone."[115]

Price wanted to be a bit more formal about reporting the success or failure of the experiment though. He knew the world was watching and he wanted research to support his claims, so the Harvard Business School tracked his results. They reported in 2018 that Gravity Payments's revenue had tripled, their customer base doubled, and their staff grew by 70%. Their employee turnover was cut in half. They also had some less common metrics to report, like that the amount of staff who'd had babies grew ten times, and that 70% of their employees had paid down debt. Ten times more employees were able to buy homes, and their 401(k) contributions grew by 155%. Their highest paid to lowest paid employee ratio had once been 33 to 1, and it dropped to 4 to 1. Gravity's head of marketing said that they've been able to thrive despite their higher labor costs, because they aren't just competing on price. "No robots, no telephone trees. Instead, real people are our infrastructure."

If you're out there saying that people are the most important part of your business, you have to act like you mean that. Making 260 times as much as your average employee, instead of passing on some of those record profits to them, isn't really sending the message that you view them as all that important.

Doing something good can inspire others to do something good. Megan Driscoll, the CEO of Pharmalogics Recruiting, saw what Price did at Gravity Payments and decided to bump their starting pay by 33%. They saw their revenue go up $8.3 million, added 26 employees, and in what's becoming a theme here, improved their employee retention. They saw better work from their employees, who recruited more qualified candidates for their clients. Employees do

---

115 Lucy Rock, "Dan Price: The CEO Who Took a Pay Cut to Give His Staff a $70k Minimum Wage," *The Guardian*, November 29, 2015, theguardian.com/society/2015/nov/29/future-of-work-dan-price-gravity-ceo-cut-own-pay-to-give-staff-increased-minum-wage/.

better work, and they're more likely to stay at a company, when they feel valued.

Dr. Bronner's, the soap company with an essay on every bottle, knows that they need their employees. They've tied their CEO salary to the wage of their lowest paid employees, and set a 5 to 1 cap. Bronner's is a family owned business, and they say that the cap ensures a more fair distribution of income within their company. Their highest paid executive earns around $240,000 a year. The company is certainly successful, making $170 million in revenue in 2022. Starting pay for regular employees is $25 per hour, around $47,000 annually. They direct any surplus profits toward charitable organizations and providing their employees with childcare support. They've fostered a positive work culture, aligned their practices with the company's value of equity and sustainability, and continue to make quite a lot of money. "An ethical company should pay a fair salary and good benefits and enable people to make ends meet on the wages they receive," CEO David Bronner said in Entrepreneur magazine, adding, "We're really trying to set an example of just being reasonable."[116]

This is the crux of our burned out population's plea to the people making these decisions about our work lives—just be reasonable. In the amount of work you're meting out, in the compensation we get for doing it, in the policies you enact that can make employees feel like assets instead of cogs.

Companies who do succeed while sharing their profits show that extreme pay ratios are a choice. These changes inspire more change, and our support for companies that are fair and respect their workforce will encourage other companies to follow suit. We are simply asking that these companies be reasonable. And if you know your labor history, you will know that there will come a time when we are no longer asking.

---

116 Sherin Shebu, "This Company Caps CEO Pay Depending on How Much Its Lowest-Paid Employee Makes," *Entrepreneur*, July 1, 2024, entrepreneur.com/business-news/dr-bronners-ceo-salary-cap-based-on-lowest-employee-wage/476435.

Cooperative Models

When we think of a business, most of us are thinking of investor-owned corporations. And while you may think that their primary goal is to make products or offer a service, it's not. Their primary goal is to generate value for the shareholders that they are beholden to. They may make customers happy or benefit society along the way, but that isn't the goal in itself. They keep running because they are making money for their shareholders.

By contrast, cooperatives run differently, because their primary goal is not the same. They have no shareholders to consider, because the company isn't owned by investors, it is owned by its own members. The people who are doing the day-to-day work are the same people who decide how to make a product or provide a service, and they are the same people who will decide what they'll do with the profits. One member, one vote. But what does a cooperative business model have to do with your burnout? As it turns out, a sustainable and equitable workplace is a huge benefit for these owner-operators.

Cooperatives are often the best choice available, so much so that they seem to have sprung up out of necessity. Workers have done something for themselves that no one else was going to do for them. In 2001, when Argentina's economy collapsed, many of its factory owners intended to close. Workers took them over instead, and they ran the factories themselves. They got to keep their jobs, the factory kept making products, and they continued their impact on the community.

Sometimes cooperatives are built because employees are frustrated with the way that their workplace or industry is handling things, and the best way to resolve that is through greater ownership. Brianna Wettlaufer left iStock to form Stocksy United for this reason. Like iStock, it's an image provider, but *Modern Retail* reports that Stocksy United is owned and operated by over nine hundred photographers.[117] Most stock image services, including iStock, pay royalties of somewhere between 15% and 45% to their contributors. But the Network for Business Sustainability reports that at Stocksy, 50 to 70% of all licenses go directly to the people who created the photos.[118] They've decided to operate differently than the rest of the industry, and they say that the sense of community and ownership that this creates drives everyone to make the highest quality imagery. It makes sense that photographers would be inclined to up their game, knowing that the majority of the profits will be going back into their own pockets.

Some of the increased interest in a cooperative model comes from generational change. Nonprofit Quarterly reports that baby boomers own around half of all small businesses, and they don't all have plans for a successor when they retire. If their own kids aren't interested in taking over the business, most of them end up simply closing.[119] Melissa Hoover, the director of Democracy at Work Institute, encourages those small business owners to sell the company to their workers instead, reports Modern Retail. Helping these businesses to continue on isn't just important for the employees who work there, but for the surrounding communities. Transitioning into a cooperative means maintaining stability in the local economy. It makes such a meaningful difference that some cities, like Miami, San Francisco, and Berkeley are creating programs to help business owners make the transition.

For many, though, a cooperative model just makes the most sense to them. When Ian Thomas noticed that he was competing with another freelancer for clients, he thought that it made much more sense to go into business together instead. They formed Tailspinners, turning a loose association of freelancers into a cooperative business.

---

117 Michael Waters, "Why Ocean Spray's Cooperative Business Model Is Getting a Second Look," *ModernRetail*, October 20, 2022, modernretail.co/retailers/why-ocean-sprays-cooperative-business-model-is-getting-a-second-look/.

118 Nathan Schneider, "How to Adopt a Cooperative Business Model," NBS.net, September 9, 2020, nbs.net/how-to-adopt-a-cooperative-business-model/.

119 Ibid

Freelancing can be a lonely business, and banding together gives them support creatively, emotionally, socially, and financially. They sign NDAs as a company, instead of as individuals, so that they can talk about clients and projects together. Instead of each freelancer paying for their own accounting systems, websites, PR, and the like, those are shared costs and shared resources. When someone is out sick, someone else is available to cover and answer emails for them. There is strength in numbers, and everyone in the cooperative shares their networks, their client lists, and their skill sets.

In game development, film, television, and other project-based industries, it's common practice to hire some short-term freelancers and contractors. When the project is finished, all of those people are out of a job and move on to the next one. It's a gig economy, and there's no security for workers in it. Tailspinners keeps a deep bench of talent, and they do add freelancers as they grow their client list. But they add them on sustainably, so that they aren't letting people go when projects wrap. They take on new projects together, as a team, instead of everyone scattering to find their next gig.

After the success of the game *Night in the Woods*, Scott Benson of The Glory Society was faced with a decision of how to move forward. He, and the other Glory Society members, had worked in the service industry and as struggling artists, so they were very familiar with the dynamic of being a disposable employee. They already had a history of projects that were run by consensus, but decided to make it official as a legal entity in 2019. Benson says that a lot of people on the team have political ideals that went into the decision to go cooperative, but it's really about how the model benefits all of them. Efficiency, transparency, accountability, and having control over the company is good for every employee.

Ian MacKaye, who started Dischord Records, said in an interview with Paul Brannigan in 2014 that it was hard for him to imagine creative control being any kind of reality if he were to sign on with a major label. He was offered some fairly enormous chunks of cash to do so, but as he says, once you are an object of investment, people will do everything they can to maximize their returns on you. You're beholden to the people giving you the money, as in an investor-owned business model. But when you've formed a cooperative, you're the person with the money.

In all of these cases—from Argentinian factory workers to the guy from Minor Threat—workers saw the benefit in running their operations collectively. The growth-at-all-costs model that dominates our economy is looking increasingly unstable, and that drives interest in finding a better way of doing things. Worker cooperatives create quality jobs where employees can build real wealth, while they provide essential products and services.

When the people who are at the lowest level of the organization are still able to be represented at the highest level of governance—one member, one vote—those companies will almost always choose the path that leads to the most security for their workers, which makes their operation sustainable. They're able to make decisions that are in their own best interests, setting wages and health care benefits, even deciding on hours of operation that promote better work-life balance. When the company posts record profits, cooperatives distribute that surplus back to the workers, which you may recognize as the thing that we are all asking of our billionaire CEO class. You are the company, so if it does well, then you do well. There is a common misconception that this kind of structure can only work with a small business, but even very large corporations can work with a cooperative model. Cranberry farmers have both owned and operated Ocean Spray since its founding. Ace Hardware, Cabot Creamery, and Blue Diamond Almonds are very large enterprises, and they're all cooperatives.

Sustainability is one benefit which is important in a business, but there are many selling points to a cooperative business model. The most obvious benefit is a more equitable distribution of profits, but it can also be a lower cost way to start a business. Volunteerism and sweat equity can reduce your initial costs. I've spent some time here saying that it's unfair to expect workers to volunteer their time, and when you're working for free to build someone else's empire, it is. But with a cooperative, you may be volunteering time to build something that you will co-own. The benefits of your labor won't go to CEOs or shareholders, they will go to you and the people who work beside you.

A cooperative model can also change the way that the people in your community see you and your business. Customers often view cooperatives as being more worthy of their trust and loyalty than investor-owned businesses, as a space that cares about their workers and their community.

And they're often more resilient businesses. Because of the sense of shared sacrifice, and a greater aversion to big risks that could hurt their workforce if they backfire, Network for Business Sustainability states that cooperatives have a lower chance of failure.[120] Investor owned companies may tell you that we're all in this together, but in a cooperative, you truly are.

With all of these benefits, you may be wondering if a cooperative structure is the best thing for your own company. But how do they actually work? If there's no boss, exactly, how does anything get done?

Larger cooperatives, like Ocean Spray or Ace Hardware, do still have managers and boards of directors who oversee operations. So how is that different from any other company? For one, those higher-ups are elected by the workers, and the type of hierarchy that makes the best sense for the company is also something that the workers collectively decide. For another, while there is still a hierarchy to many cooperative businesses, the distribution of power is quite different.

Typically, an investor-owned corporation will have a boss at the top, with various managers below them, and employees below them. Even in a workplace where you feel a sense of ownership and autonomy around the work that you do, your boss is still the one

120 Ibid

with all the power. You don't decide what your hours are, or how much you'll be paid. In a cooperative, you may still have a boss who is responsible for administrative tasks and overseeing the work being done, but that boss has the same power that you do. Decisions about hours and wages, even deadlines, are made collectively by everyone, and it changes the dynamic of how you work together. There is greater accountability, greater participation. Importantly, there's also greater job security, because collective decisions are based on not having to lay yourself off.

Ted Anderson of Pixel Pushers Union 512 explains that their indie studio—a worker-owned game development team—votes management into their positions. In a 2019 GDC (Game Developers Conference) panel, Anderson says that there isn't a salary tied to that position, so it becomes less about holding onto that power than it is about actually being a good manager.[121] It also means that it's easier for managers to step down from their positions if they feel they aren't effective at it, without worrying about the loss in pay. At Pixel Pushers, everyone starts with the same base salary, and everyone gets an equal share in the profits of the game they work on.

Cooperatives are not all sunshine and roses, they are still a business, and complications and inter-office problems still arise. When something is everyone's responsibility, it's also no one's responsibility. There are what Steve Filby of Motion Twin calls in that same GDC panel the "ugly jobs." Somebody has to do the dishes, somebody has to take out the trash, and somebody has to tell somebody else that they're fired. How do you fire someone in a zero hierarchy co-op? Like everything else, it's by democratic vote. Because it's harder to fire someone in this kind of environment, hiring is taken very seriously, and cooperatives may hire someone to a temporary contract before they officially join the team. Everyone has a say in everything, but

121 Scott Benson, Ted Anderson, Ian Thomas, and Steve Filby, "Embracing the Co-Op Studio Model in Indie Games," GDC Vault, March 2019, gdcvault.com/play/1025700/Embracing-the-Co-Op-Studio.

with a larger co-op, that can mean a lot of opinions to manage. It's a bit like getting twelve people to order a pizza.

As a cooperative gets larger, you have to have more rigorous communication standards to make sure that everyone stays involved, but you may have to limit team sizes so that everyone can come to an agreement on the proverbial pizza toppings. Studios may instead have a horizontal organization, but vertical deployment, Scott Benson explains in their GDC panel on embracing the co-op model.[122] Maybe that means that the creative director acts as the creative director, and everyone doesn't vote on the artwork. But instead of the creative director unilaterally deciding on the deadlines that designers and illustrators will follow, everyone still discusses and votes on that, so that no one is surprised by a deadline or a schedule change.

Juggling all of these personalities and opinions can mean more rules and systems to keep everything running smoothly. Filby says that their studio tracks time very carefully, but not for the reason most companies do. Their concern is that their people are prone to work far too many hours, which leads to the crunch culture that's so prevalent in game design. They may have a discussion when too many people have been working too many hours, and decide to take a week off to compensate. Each company has to look at the work that they do, and decide together on the best way to do it, and these considerations may change over time as they grow.

There are a multitude of ways that you can choose to run a cooperative, and the wonderful thing about them is that the people who are doing the work get to decide those things. As a group, you can determine what works best for the people in your cooperative, and for the kind of work that you do. You can create something that runs in a sustainable way, that's equitable for every worker who contributes to the success of the company.

Cooperatives can form for different reasons, whether it's the only way to keep a company afloat or the owner simply doesn't want

122 Ibid

to be the owner anymore. But at the end of the day, cooperatives exist because that model was the best way to move forward. Benson dreaded the idea of being someone else's boss, and of structuring the labor and relationships of a company. With the cooperative model, he's set up something that solves a lot of the issues he sees. Legally, every member of The Glory Society owns The Glory Society. They all work for themselves, and they all work for each other.

There is more than one way forward to build a better way to work. But one big piece of the puzzle is understanding that we don't have to work the way that we have been, simply because that's the system that is in place. We don't have to work forty hours a week, just because we have for so long. We don't have to give every bit of surplus profit to our CEOs. We don't have to have CEOs at all.

If you are starting or already running a business, you can build that business differently. Creating a better work culture requires this belief that things can be better, and the will to fight for that. We need to reclaim our downtime, our mental space, and our ability to gather with our communities to see that change is possible.

To save ourselves, we must save each other. And to do that, we need solidarity with our fellow workers.

CONCLUSION: SOLIDARITY

So what have we learned?

That hustle culture is directly leading to our widespread burnout.

That it goes against the way that our brains are built to work and devalues the people and the care work they do in our communities.

That our views about work and morality, our need for identity and meaning, are behind much of our need to constantly be working.

How the way that jobs have shifted their risk onto us drives the precarity that makes us feel like we can't stop.

But importantly, we've also learned that this culture is not inevitable. It's not unchangeable, and we can fight back against the tide of overwork.

We can unite against burnout, realizing that no one truly benefits from increasingly longer hours.

We can opt out of glorifying this culture of total work and embrace slowness and self-care and boundaries.

And we can save ourselves from burnout by saving each other.

Still, I have saved what's arguably the most important concept when talking about saving us all from burnout culture for last.

Solidarity. Individual choice can't be our only means of resistance, we simply can't change an entire culture alone. We may talk about the choices that we are able to make individually, and we should do that. I've spent a few thousand words on it myself, here. Just because biking to work won't undo the damage that corporations do to our climate doesn't mean that there aren't benefits to biking to work, to an individual and to their community. But we also have to look critically at the options that are available to each of us, which are often pretty limited. Privilege grants some of us more choices than others, and some of those choices can come at another person's expense. We have to fight for each other, and that requires solidarity.

It also requires us to believe that real change is possible, in a time when that can feel like a pipe dream. There is an annual global survey called the Edelman Trust Barometer, and it measures public confidence in our institutions. In 2025, they report that distrust is society's default emotion; we are fueled by fear and grievance.[123] We work for a society that we don't have any faith in. And the more work we do and the better work we do, the worse our jobs have become. We are stressed out, burned out, and tired out, increasing wealth for people who are already incredibly wealthy at the expense of our own well-being.

If we don't have faith in our society, how can we have any investment in it? How can we even believe change is possible, let alone fight for it?

That requires some information about how movements happen. How they are formed, how they grow, and how they are sustained. A community, a group with shared experiences, creates that belief. When people join groups, like the Democratic Socialists of America (DSA), a union, or a LGBTQ+ rights organization, they are able to see small wins happening, and the potential for larger change will then seem within research. You believe that change is possible, because you're

123 Edelman Trust Barometer, 25th anniversary edition, edelman.com/trust/2025/trust-barometer/.

surrounded by other people who do. For a culture to change, people have to believe that change is even a possibility, and it helps to be embedded in a social group that makes the change easier.

In *The Power of Habit*, Carles Duhigg talks about how movements begin because of social patterns, grow because of the community, and sustain because a leader gives those people new habits. With all of these together, a movement can become self-propelling and reach critical mass. With apologies to Gandhi, be the change you wish to see in your workplace.

Movements don't simply happen through an individual act of defiance; the Montgomery bus boycott didn't simply spring up out of thin air because Rosa Parks didn't want to move. Similar arrests hadn't spontaneously started any social movements. But a friend of Parks' needed a case to use so that they could fight Montgomery's bus laws, and they asked her specifically if they could fight her arrest in court.

She was a good choice, because she was well-known and liked in her community. We all have a sense of moral outrage when we see injustice. But when our friend is hurt, when a pillar of our community is hurt, that outrage is much greater, and it's enough to overcome the inertia that makes social movements hard to organize. There is a sense that you have an obligation to protect your community—basically, peer pressure put to good use.

Movements don't happen because everyone suddenly decides to change at once, and Duhigg says that weak ties are just as important as strong ones in building them. Strong ties are your close friends and family, and it can be a small group. Weak ties include your acquaintances, friends of friends, your larger community, the people you work with. Including those weak ties builds a larger social net, and it can turn a small protest into a society wide movement.

Movements like a boycott don't happen by coincidence, and it's also not a great coincidence that so many social movements began when we were all quarantined during the pandemic. Most of the time, our jobs keep us too busy and tired to agitate for change. It's like when your second grade teacher would give you some worksheets to do during the last week of school, it's a time-wasting task to keep you from bothering them.

If we had the time for deep thought, for organizing with our neighbors, we might decide that the point of our lives isn't making rich people richer, but in caring for each other. Labor isn't virtuous in itself, but labor can still be a force for good.

What about labor that helps others? Businesses that put human dignity at the center of their culture? What if we reimagined the nature of what work is? Saving ourselves, and each other, requires us to change the way that we think about the morality of work, and about what is and isn't politically possible. It requires us to spend time with each other, to see how much we have in common. It also requires us to build collective power.

Systemic problems require systemic solutions. You can't save the Earth from climate change by going vegan, and you can't singlehandedly change the way that corporations are run. But we can make changes collectively. The only way to make change is to have leverage. It may take legislation that makes a company responsible for more risk again, and mandates that profits produced by an employees' work should, at least in part, come back to them. This used to be common in America.

Unions are also a crucial step toward changing the power dynamics around work. The system, as it stands, is working for a lot of people. Causing problems and then selling solutions to those problems is wildly profitable, and those who make all the money have no incentive to change it.

Deregulation and union-busting allow capitalism to be as ruthless as it wants.

Corporations wouldn't work so hard to bust unions if collective bargaining weren't so effective. Historically, they have put a great deal of effort into busting unions, as workers have put just as much effort into fighting for their rights.

The Luddites, often maligned as people who don't understand or value technology, were a group that understood strength in numbers. After the British government passed legislation to prohibit trade unions in the 1800s, mill owners introduced more machines to their factories and cut wages for workers. The Luddites fought back, planning coordinated attacks on mill frameworks.

They weren't against the idea of progress, but they saw how technology was being used to limit their rights, and they used a number of tactics to fight back. They wrote letters for better wages and ending child labor, and earned solidarity from their local communities. Eventually, mill owners were afraid that their communities would turn on them.

The Luddites questioned technology, and when it didn't serve them, they resisted it. Slow living, quiet quitting, resisting efficiency as an end goal—all these things can be seen as modern Luddism, as illustrated by *The Nib.*[124]

We can be inspired not only by what they fought for, but how they fought for it. They broke the machines that put workers out of jobs, something that many people in industries threatened by AI can relate to. In San Francisco, security robots were sent out to harass the homeless, and people intentionally damaged them. One was covered with barbeque sauce and wrapped in a tarp. People slashed the tires of driverless cars after one killed a woman in Arizona. Computer science students work to develop tools to keep AI from stealing artists' work. We are breaking the machines that threaten our rights, as Luddites broke mill frameworks before us. We work collectively for change.

---

124 Tom Humberstone, "I'm a Luddite (and So Can You!)", *The Nib,* July 17, 2023, thenib.com/im-a-luddite/.

What we cannot do is simply wait around and hope that companies will do the right thing, even though some of them do. For many corporations, our ability to burn out and keep on going is one of our greatest assets. Even when we are trying to help workers who are burned out, much of the effort goes into making them feel better (which is good, and useful). Little effort is made to actually change the nature of their work, so that they don't get burned out in the first place. As Michael Leiter says in Scientific American, wellness programs help people to tolerate their situation rather than change it.[125] What if, instead, we focused on changing the actual culture of work?

Change doesn't have to be big to make a difference. Small changes can have a domino effect on work culture. Paul O'Neill became the CEO of Alcoa in 1987, and he was singularly committed to worker safety. It was his top priority, and it was something that both his workers and his shareholders could agree on. But he didn't come in with a four-hundred page plan to upend everything about the company; he just created a policy where every time an injury happened, there would be a report that presented a plan to prevent that injury from happening again. And it had to be done within twenty-four hours. That's it. One policy. But that change created other changes down the line.

Reporting an injury within twenty-four hours meant that everyone had to be communicating, and that everyone was actively on the lookout for potential safety hazards and ways to solve them. Duhigg describes the work culture at Alcoa in *The Power of Habit*, stating that they had an injury rate that was 1/20 the US average at the time—O'Neill's policy was very effective. And though he made no promises that improving safety would raise their profits, it did. A theme throughout this book has been that doing the right thing for workers also turns out to be great for business. Focusing on safety—which is the right thing to do in a factory—made their workers more efficient. Focusing their attention on potential problems made for a

125 Dönges and Bushwick, "A Four-Day Workweek Reduces Stress."

better quality product. They even saved money and time when their workers were absent less, because they weren't getting injured all the time. Duhigg writes that O'Neill retired in 2000, and Alcoa's annual net income had increased five times from when he started.[126]

Focusing on a small win can help other habits to flourish, and they can convince people that bigger achievements are possible. In the early 1970s, the Library of Congress classified books about the gay liberation movement as "abnormal sexual relations, including sex crimes." Gay rights organizations campaigned for them to change that. For all the things that gay rights organizations had to fight for then, this seems like a very small win. But when they achieved it, news spread, and those organizations could cite that victory as the reason they started fundraising drives. Gay politicians ran for office citing that win as what had inspired them to run. If we could do that, what else could we do? In 1973, the APA rewrote their definition of homosexuality, and that win paved the way for anti-discrimination laws. Progress is not linear, it's a snowball effect.

Progress comes from solidarity, and solidarity comes from an idea of common goods. But it's an idea that our society has moved away from. In *Capitalism 3.0*, Peter Barnes, entrepreneur and environmentalist, argues that we need to cultivate common wealth in order to balance out private wealth. That we should include not only things like air, water, ecosystems, and language in the list of things that we share, but also science, tech, and legal arrangements. That we should create a new set of institutions to make capitalism more environmentally conscious, and more protective of the people who live and work in it. Barnes argues that these natural and social assets are our joint inheritance, and that they belong to us all equally.[127]

I am old enough to remember that the idea of bottling and selling water seemed absolutely mad. Nestlé doesn't own water, who would

126 Charles Duhigg. *The Power of Habit: Why We Do What We Do in Life and Business.* Random House, 2012.

127 Peter Barnes, *Capitalism 3.0: A Guide to Reclaiming the Commons* (Berrett-Koehler Publishing, 2006).

ever pay for that? Creating a common good so that we can all benefit from its use isn't a new idea, but an old one. We have libraries, public schools, and fire departments. The Nature Conservancy holds more than fifteen million acres of land, and protects them for everyone. The Alaska Permanent Fund invests part of their oil revenues on behalf of every resident, and it pays out yearly equal dividends to them. Of course, this all requires a belief that, say, Alaska's oil doesn't belong to a private entity, but to the people. That our resources belong to us equally. That we are all in this together.

Corporations and governments tend to maximize short-term gain, but common property trusts have long timelines and a responsibility to future generations. We also have common things that we share on smaller scales, like community gardens, simple public spaces, and municipal Wi-Fi. Trusts for our watersheds or local habitats. Little free libraries, and public pantries, and events in our spaces that we open to our community. What all these have in common, from the largest to the smallest, is common ownership, inclusivity, and a desire to put future generations first. This is the kind of mindset that is required to make a culture better: that every person is deserving of the benefits of their community, and that we all have to work together toward that future.

To fight for ourselves, we must fight for each other. And to do that, we must believe that every person deserves the same things that we do.

Yes, immigrants.

Yes, people of color.

Yes, the disabled.

Yes, the unhoused.

Whoever you're thinking of, the answer is yes, even them.

Often, we want to believe that other people's suffering is their own fault. That their lives are the way they are because of the choices that they've made. We cling to this belief because it allows us to think that bad things can't happen to us. If someone is only living in poverty because they've made bad choices, then I never have to worry about living in poverty, because I simply will make better choices.

But if we know that people living in poverty do so because of bad systems that work against them, because of rampant income inequality, low wages, and unaffordable housing, then we are aware that it could easily happen to anyone. It could happen to us.

During the pandemic, people seemed to be almost pleased that it was affecting people with preexisting health conditions the most. *Thank God, that means it can't happen to me.* But all of us are closer than we think to our own preexisting conditions. I didn't have an autoimmune disease until I did. And I didn't acquire it through poor choices, or bad diet, or anything other than an unfortunate bit of bad luck. We can't fight for our fellow humans if we believe that they don't deserve the help. We can't fight for our fellow humans if we think that we're somehow better than they are. Solidarity isn't charity—it's the understanding that we really are all in this together. It's recognizing how connected we are, how we are linked together. That when one of us suffers, all of us suffer.

We can't dig ourselves out of the problems that hustle culture has caused for us alone. What we can do is change our mindset about what our brains and bodies need to thrive, separate our sense of self and dignity from our work, and see the value in leisure and deep thought—and these things are important. It's necessary for more people to reconsider their relationship to work in their lives, and the push to optimize every bit of our day toward being a more productive worker. If we don't change that mindset, there's not a way forward in changing our culture. Opting out of those views, setting healthy boundaries, and taking actual care of ourselves can do us all a world of good and help us to build a life that's meaningful.

But ultimately, we have to work together to change the system if we hope to create a work culture that protects the health and dignity of every worker.

To reclaim our solidarity to build something better, something that works for us all. To look for those who are already working, and join them.

To prevent not only my own burnout, but yours.

To pledge our loyalty not to our bosses, but to each other.

To allow ourselves and others to be fully human in a culture that seeks only to extract our value as workers.

To use what power we have individually to structure work in a more ethical way, and to use our collective power to make it universal.

We have more power together than we do alone. We are society, we are labor, we are culture. We can change.

We're all we've got, and we're all we need.

For as little as $15/month, you can support a small, independent publisher and get every book that we publish—delivered to your doorstep!

www.Microcosm.Pub/BFF

More Books about Self-Empowerment anb Fighting Capitalism

UNF#CK YOUR WORTH

OVERCOME YOUR MONEY EMOTIONS, VALUE YOUR OWN LABOR, AND MANAGE FINANCIAL FREAK-OUTS IN A CAPITALIST HELLSCAPE

FAITH G. HARPER, PhD, LPC-S, ACS, A